Dedicated to my husband, my children, and all those in my family who allowed me to find my way and loved me in spite of the long journey, and to Jesse who never left my side.

Table of Contents

introduction

Kentucky/Missouri Border
1971

The crash happened almost in slow motion. I didn't realize what was happening until it was over. We were traveling in a caravan, four large family cars one after the other. It was a two-lane road that wove through the hills and countryside along the Mississippi River near the Kentucky and Missouri border.

I was filthy, covered in dirt and mud sitting in the back seat of our four-door family car. My sister was beside me. Mom and Dad sat up front. My little brother had been bouncing from the front seat to the back until my sister and I had threatened him. One more trip over the seat, and he would be riding in the back window pressed against the glass.

Mom had intervened, insisting my brother sit still. She had started singing and encouraged us all to join her, hoping the song would distract my kid brother. It had been a great day. Our yearly picnic with friends (that my little brother referred to as "the good people," and that I had known my entire life) had ended in a cloud of dirt and dust. Altogether, there were ten dirty and exhausted kids being dusted and wiped down until our frustrated mothers gave in. They decided we could sit on newspapers for the trip home to save the interior of the cars.

We had spent the day at a park we knew almost as well as the countryside around our homes. The yearly trip had been a tradition for our little group for as long as any of us could remember. Just before we were scheduled to leave, my friends and I had discovered a hillside trail that had worn away just enough to create the perfect earthen slide. By the time the cars were loaded and our parents were calling for us to leave, we were all so covered in thick crusted dirt there was no way we could be properly cleaned for the car ride home.

I was just starting to feel a little sleepy. Mom was still singing, my sister was curled up in the seat behind my dad, and my little brother had finally settled down with his head resting against my dad's right arm.

I had just scooted down in my seat, propped my knees up on the seat behind my Mom, and was about to shut my eyes. Mom's song was now fading to a soft hum. The melody was familiar. It was a song we had sung that morning in church before leaving for our annual picnic at Columbus Park.

Now the peace and quiet was shattered. My mom was no longer humming, but she was breathing. We could hear her moaning. Her side of the car had taken the hardest hit. The car was headed straight for us, but Dad had swerved into the oncoming lane just enough to lessen the blow from the head-on collision.

The driver was flying. It was much later before we realized that the occupants in the other car were a husband and wife. He had been drinking and she was pregnant with a baby due any day. They had lost control of their car and weaved in and out of our little caravan barely missing the other cars, hitting us before flipping several times, and finally coming to rest against a tree down the hill.

Dad was talking, asking if we were all right. My little brother had slid out of his seat and under my dad's legs in the front seat— easily the only place he could have been protected from the impact. Everything else in the front seat was a jumbled mess. The entire floorboard had collapsed on my Mom's legs. We learned later that one leg was broken, the other twisted and bruised. The dash was against her chest and glass was everywhere. The steering wheel had hit my Dad in the face. You could already see the swelling in his jaw as he quickly pulled us from the car.

Everyone's attention turned to my mother. Since we were so far out in the country, it was decided we would not wait for the ambulance, but take her to the hospital in one of the other cars. I was so young I don't remember anything about the other car. I was worried about my mom. She was going to be fine, but I had never been so frightened.

At the hospital we learned the occupants of the other car had been thrown from the vehicle as it flipped. They both survived but their unborn child didn't make it. Later that night, I wondered why we had survived and the baby had not. My best friend was the one who made me think for the first time that sometimes God is hard to understand. No one doubted that God had protected us, especially my little brother. If he had slid under Mom's legs instead of Dad's, he would have been crushed. Why did God do what He did? Jesse seemed to understand things like that better than I ever could. He said God didn't cause the wreck. Yes, He had allowed it to happen, but sometimes His plans have to be protected from what the world can throw in our path. That was why we had survived a crash that should have killed us all. Obviously, God had plans for us.

Jesse

Childhood friendships are something I don't think anyone appreciates until they grow old. It is on the look back that you see the way those special friends wove through every part of your life and you begin to appreciate them for what they were.

Jesse was a friend like that, always there, always loyal, and always taken for granted. Honestly, if we both had not been such social outcasts, I might not have noticed him at all.

My first vivid memories of Jesse were in 1969. We had just received word that a close friend had been killed in Vietnam. I remember the shock and the disbelief, but mostly I remember Jesse, telling me through tears that it is okay to be sad, angry, and simply at a loss to understand something as tragic as war. Years later, we talked about senseless loss when news came that a friend had been killed by a drunk driver while walking home from school.

Jesse was there to help me sort out the tough things we all see when hearts are too young to understand, and to rejoice over the daily miracles and blessings that so often go unnoticed without a friend to share them.

Jesse was never more important in my life than while I was young, especially as I watched friends live the life I wanted, but never thought I could have. I talked with Jesse night after night. I would dream and he would listen. He looked past the surface to the person I really was and believed the dream was possible. But what did he know? He didn't fit in either.

As I grew up, Jesse was always there. Looking back, I don't know how I would have survived without him. That is why it is so hard to think about the times in my life when I nearly forgot he was there.

chapter 1

Western Kentucky 1977

Growing up, it seemed like every day ended talking to Jesse. Sometimes I would fall asleep right in the middle of a conversation. We always had something to sort out, work out, or just air out. When I was young, he begged me to not give in to the discouragement I received from a handful of tormentors that stalked the halls in my school. But I was such an easy target. I was an oddity, especially for a girl, taller and bigger than everyone I knew. I was a gifted speaker and I could sing, but I shied away from the spotlight. I was too afraid of what others would say.

Jesse encouraged and counseled me every day. The year my sister became popular was no different. Almost overnight (it was actually over the summer), everything changed. She lost weight, worked on her tan, and got a new haircut. The transformation was amazing. She suddenly went from a slightly shorter version of me with darker hair, to someone who looked more like my beautiful cousins everyone fussed over and flirted with.

Her sudden popularity led to dating, and dating very quickly—much too quickly—led to talk of marriage. We grew up in rural Kentucky. Our parents were, and still are, farmers. We are "country" to the core. It's not unheard of for teenagers to talk of marriage as early as sixteen or seventeen, especially back in the day. Still, with my sister, it all seemed to be moving way too fast. I was just getting used to the idea of her having a boyfriend when they announced their engagement.

I don't remember thinking it was a bad idea, just one that came about too quickly. She seemed happy, her fiancé was a nice enough guy, but what did I know? I was fourteen! Then I remembered she had just turned seventeen. Was anyone paying attention? That was the question Jesse asked over and over. He had a ton of them. "Who is this guy? Do we know much about his family? Does he have a job? How about God, does he believe in God? You know, that is something you really need to consider."

I told Jesse to talk with my sister if he was so concerned. Of course, he quickly reminded me how stubborn she was. Even more stubborn than me, if that is possible. We all knew that unless she asked for someone's advice, she would not only ignore the unsolicited information, but she would go out of her way to do exactly the opposite, if possible.

He was right. She was stubborn, just like me. We were so much alike, and still are. Thinking back, I know now we also shared that same restless longing for someone to love us who didn't have to. Don't get me wrong, we grew up in a family full of love, but outside, in a world full of peers and school hallways, we watched and dreamed. It seemed like everyone had what we wanted so badly. What would it be like to be popular, to be liked, maybe even loved someday? To be loved by someone who didn't sit across the supper table from us. I knew how she felt. She had been lonely too.

Less than one year later

She never looked more beautiful as the days zipped by. We went to wedding showers and bridal teas. She found the perfect dress and spent days daydreaming of the home she would share with her handsome groom. I barely blinked and I was walking down the aisle just in front of her. Moments later, there she was, beautiful, but so young, and something just didn't seem right.

She didn't have that wedding glow I thought every bride would have. She seemed uncertain. Everyone said it was just nerves.

Years later, she confessed it was that feeling of being trapped, like she had walked into something and there was no way to turn around. Mom said she had sensed it too and had told her she didn't have to go through with it, but my sister wouldn't listen.

Barely a moment passed and they were introduced as Mr. and Mrs. If you have never been to a country wedding, especially back in the day, we didn't play around. Weddings were a quick "I do. Do you?" Then, if everyone was in agreement, we would celebrate with punch, cake, and salted peanuts. And for formal weddings, little bowls of butter mints too. The entire affair seemed to be over before it began. As she left in a shower of rice, I could not help but feel a little afraid for my sister when they jumped in the car and drove away.

chapter 2

Transformations

Just six months after she said, "I do," she didn't anymore. I soon learned the fear I had for my sister was not for her physical being, but for her heart. I think the heartbreak left her a little numb inside. Her husband's betrayal was so deep and cold that no one blamed her when the divorce came more quickly than the romance. Everything that had changed in a blink, changed again in a half-blink as she tried to start over. She was in the middle of her senior year in high school. Dad wanted her to focus on getting through the year and then she could go to college. She loved math, maybe she could make that her major.

Things tried to return to normal—normal pre-boyfriend, pre-husband—but they couldn't. She was really popular now. Still beautiful, she was the toast of the town in a way. She had lived more in one year than most of her classmates had in a lifetime. She put on a brave face, but I could tell she was torn up inside. Jesse noticed it too. She was the subject of many late night talks, but the conclusion was always the same. She had to work this out on her own.

Her senior year ended and my junior year began. Watching from the sidelines, I had concluded that life seemed much more exciting "slim and beautiful" than "big and awkward." Granted, the horrible marriage thing held no appeal, but everyone said my sister and I were so much alike. It was worth a try. I thought, if I worked out and dieted, maybe my social life would improve too. Besides, my basketball coach had made it clear, get in shape or don't play ball. I decided if I wanted a life outside of the cornfield, I needed to see if I could turn into a swan as well.

Jesse was the only one not on board with my summer makeover plan. He agreed that getting healthy was a great idea, but thought it was a very bad idea to assume losing a few pounds and getting a new haircut was going to change my social standing. Still, I would not be convinced. I was certain this would work.

All summer, I ate right and exercised every day. I loved to swim, but quickly discovered I liked to run as well. Stunned by this new revelation, I went all in. Nothing would keep me from my daily workout. I had great stamina. I was already accustomed to the heat from years of working on the farm. My mom and dad would scold me every time they caught me running during the heat of the day. That was a hot summer with several one-hundred-degree days. I loved it.

I would run and sweat until everything I wore was soaked. Then barely kicking off my shoes, I would dive into the cold water. The pool was always so cold. Our water came from an underground spring and stayed cool even in the summer. I topped off the pool almost every day to keep it chilled. I can still feel the shock of the cold water as I swam laps day after day in the family pool.

Yes, we had a pool. Of course, our pool was not a typical spa facility. It was actually two rings from a grain storage bin, but you would never know it. The rings were linked together to form a figure eight and were buried in the ground with a concrete floor and patio. It was, and still is, awesome. Just a great example of what you can do with what you have if you just think on it for awhile. Something my dad is very good at and I struggle to master to this day.

Anyway, by the end of the summer I had met my goal. I was in real athletic shape, slim and, I guess, pretty. I felt pretty, so I hoped someone else would notice. Jesse was proud of me, but was still concerned. He thought I was counting too much on things changing. "It isn't that easy," he said over and over. I knew he was concerned, but my teenage patience was wearing thin. I was tired of his advice to simply ignore my peers. I was dealing with people that seemed to make a game out of tormenting any of us that didn't quite fit in. "Don't let them get to you. You are better than that," he would say until I could hear his advice echoing in my sleep.

The first week of school went okay, but Jesse was right. Things didn't seem much different. A few people commented on how great I looked, but several of my classmates made fun of me for losing weight, almost as if they were mocking me for trying. Especially one girl. I can still see her smirking. She would giggle and roll her eyes, whispering to my classmates whenever I walked by. I always felt sick when I was around her, constantly wondering what was wrong. Did I have toilet paper stuck to my shoe? Was there something ridiculous hanging from my nose? What could possibly be so amusing?

Jesse said, "Just ignore them. Don't let them get to you. You're better than..." I cut him off before he could finish. "You were right," I said. "Are you happy? Nothing's changed, including you telling me not to let it get to me! I'm sick of it being left up to me. When will it be their turn to do what's right?" I waited, but he didn't respond. He must have known I would not listen anyway. I was determined to feel sorry for myself, and even Jesse was not going to ruin that for me.

jesse

chapter 3

Crossing Lines?

I became sullen and irritable. I didn't want to deal with anything I didn't have to. I went to school, practiced basketball, and ran ever chance I had. Running let me think and clear my head, and there was a lot that I needed to clear away. Everything I hated about school—the tormentors that were still determined to make my life as miserable as possible; how irritating Jesse was. But mostly, I was really worried about my sister.

After graduation she had applied to college. Things were great for about two weeks. She was really excited about something again. The morning the letter came I saw a cloud come over her that I think is still with her a bit to this day. She had applied to one of the Christian colleges our parents wanted us to attend. They had agreed to pay our tuition if we attended a school with ties to our church. She was smart, brilliant actually, and there was no reason to think she would be rejected. But she was. The college did not allow students that were divorced to attend.

I don't think I have ever seen someone so quickly and so visibly have the wind knocked out of her sails. She went, in a moment, from a smiling, beautiful, young woman, to a dejected, hopeless soul that I know felt as though her life was over. She was trying to start over, but it was so hard. Most everyone knew she had no choice but to divorce her husband, but they still talked. Talk she would hear in bits and pieces when they thought she wasn't around.

I can't remember how many times conversations would stop as we approached. We grew accustomed to seeing guilty eyes, betraying the gossip they were sharing till we walked in. The thought of leaving and going to college, a fresh start, had given her hope. A hope that had vanished with one simple page that began, We are sorry to inform you....

I have never understood why she didn't immediately apply to a public university. Under the circumstances, I am certain our parents would have covered the tuition. She knew she would be admitted, and later was. Looking back, I think of how confused, distraught, and disappointed she must have been. It seemed as though her emotions had locked away her spirit. It was as if she could not think past one day or one hour. It was as though she was just going through the motions, one moment at a time.

She got an apartment and started working in town. She was settling into a new life. She got more beautiful every day. She had let her black hair grow long, and many compared her to the actress who played Wonder Woman on television. I think "Wonder Woman" was even her nickname for a while.

I was surprised I didn't know who she was dating. I didn't doubt for a minute that she was getting a lot of attention. I heard what the guys at my school said about her. Not necessarily kind things, but things that indicated they would love to date her.

I was still comfortably wallowing in my self-pity when I first heard about her new boyfriend. A friend in the hall at school said, "What is your sister thinking? Doesn't she know that is not allowed?" I remember thinking, what is she talking about? I could not imagine. It was bizarre.

At home later that night I knew something was up, but still couldn't begin to think of anything that would cause such a cloud to descend on everyone. Mom had been crying and, for a moment, I was worried that there had been an accident or something tragic. Mom and Dad were talking and I overheard them say, "I don't know. What if something happens to her?" Now they were scaring me. "What?" I finally said, "What is going on?" Dad told me, "It's your sister. We are just really worried about her." From the look on his face I imagined the worst till he said, "She has a new boyfriend." I thought with relief, are you kidding me, all of this drama over a new boyfriend? Then Dad added, "He's black."

At first, I still thought, "So what? What difference does that make?" Then I remembered a rally that had happened on the farm across the creek from ours just a few years earlier. The Ku Klux Klan had held a rally right next door. We had heard there was a Klan in the area, but we had all hoped it was a lie. Sometimes when you grow up as we had, sheltered from much of the world, it is hard to imagine that hate is anything but a story splattered across the television or a movie and not real life. The night of the rally, we went down to the edge of the field to see for ourselves.

We got there as they were wrapping up. There were clusters of people standing around talking, while others cleaned up, tossing trash into a fire. I remember being drawn to the large timbers still visible through the flames. I could not help but wonder what they had used to kindle their fire. I remember thinking everything looked as innocent as a community get-together or the clean up you would see after one the bonfires my parents hosted for the teens at our church. Still, the memory sent a chill down my spine. I was no longer just worried about my sister, I was truly afraid.

jesse

chapter 4

When Good Men Do Nothing

I understand so well how terrorism works. When 9-11 happened, my family already understood the feeling of fear terrorists instill in those they hate. That was the feeling that enveloped us all. Jesse and I began to talk more and more. I had stopped feeling sorry for myself; none of that seemed to matter anymore. I just simply wanted to understand.

It's funny—throughout my life Jesse was always the one to have an idea, a thought, and a sense for why things happen the way they do, but this time even Jesse didn't seem to understand. He pointed out that hatred was as old as time. The relationship between Cain and Abel was a perfect example. Jealously fueled the rage, but hatred committed the murder. Could any of us fully understand why people hate?

I think the toughest part was trying to find a reason for it all. Trying to find a reason and trying to understand why so many good people stood by and did nothing. There is a famous quote that has echoed through my mind for many years. "The only way for evil to triumph is for good men to do nothing" (Sir Edmond Burke). That was the problem. Good people, who knew what was happening, let their fear, disinterest, and maybe their own underlying bigotry keep them silent. When I think back, the whole mess was instigated by only a handful of hateful people, but those that stayed silent allowed the hate to grow into a cloud so thick that it was all we could see.

I guess we knew they were doomed from the start. My sister and her boyfriend dated for maybe a month or two, but even after the break-up, things didn't settle down. It was a scary time. We didn't know what to expect and we became more afraid every day, especially for my sister.

My sister must have felt like a child again. Mom and Dad were afraid for her to be alone. They worried about her constantly. It was finally decided that she should get out of the line of fire for a while. My uncle lived in Maine and offered her a port in the storm with his family. When she left, I don't think I had any real expectations about how long she would stay. I just knew she would be safe. As for the rest of us, we felt sure that things would calm down eventually.

My parents had scheduled a trip to Hawaii. They left just after the smoke cleared and my sister was tucked safely away up north. Things returned to a somewhat normal routine, even with my parents away.

I was still having a very hard time with the entire situation. None of it made sense. The reaction to my sister's relationship made me sick. Jesse and I had frequent talks long into the night. I lived in a very conservative and religious area and I could not begin to reconcile the hatred and the silence of those I knew professed a belief in God. How could one human, made in the image of God, hate another human formed in that same image because of the color of their skin? It made as much sense to hate someone because of hair or eye color.

My parents were away for about a week. My brother and I, according to my parents, were still too young to stay home alone, so an older cousin stayed with us while they were away. Nothing seemed out of the ordinary. Mom and Dad returned home on schedule and I thought things were fine until I saw my mom begin to cry. My cousin was explaining we had received a phone call just before they returned home. My sister was back in Kentucky. She had come home to marry the father of her unborn child.

chapter 5

Fear and Hate

Honestly, at this point, I was expecting the Klan to show up, set fire to a cross, and proceed to burn us out. I had no idea what would happen—none of us did. We had only heard stories and none of them were good. I had nightmares of classmates cornering me, shouting at me. I could not hear what they were saying, but I could see their anger. I saw the Confederate flag everywhere. It seemed to show up more and more on t-shirts, car bumpers, and flying from the back of pick-up trucks. I hated that flag. Even though the Klan also flew the Stars and Stripes, everyone knew the Confederate Battle Flag was their mantle.

I began to approach with caution anyone flying the Stars and Bars. It is really hard to explain. Maybe I was imagining it, but it was as though many of my classmates were trying to send me a message. One surely did. I can still see him. It was speech day in speech class, one of my best classes. We had not been assigned topics, we were simply told to pick something we were interested in. The big goof spoke on why the Ku Klux Klan had been a good thing when it originally started. I could not believe it any more than I could believe someone had actually scratched an "N" into the hood of my car.

When I first saw it, I tried to imagine how the scratch appeared to so closely resemble the letter. I think Jesse was the one that finally convinced me. It was not an accident, but it was so hard to believe. These were people I had known my entire life, or at least since first grade. Our school was first through twelfth grade. We didn't go to kindergarten back then, at least not in rural western Kentucky. But even before we went to school we all knew each other. Most of us were related, eventually, a distant cousin of a distant cousin. Everybody knew everybody. So who would have done such a thing?

I started running through suspects in my mind. It had probably happened during smoke break. I know that sounds ridiculous, but yes, we had a smoke break for the high school kids. This was tobacco country after all. We could be excused from classes to work in the tobacco fields. So I guess they thought if we were old enough to work with it, we were old enough to smoke it.

I knew who smoked, so it was fairly easy to narrow the suspects down to the list of people that would have had access to the cars during the break. I was starting to get a pretty good idea who was responsible. No, not the guy from my speech class, but one of his best buddies was a pack-a-day smoker. It was probably him. My first reaction was to talk to a teacher or someone in the office, but the more I thought about it, the more I knew there was no reason to say anything. No one would care. The simple truth was that a few of the teachers might have even thought it was funny.

As the news of my sister's marriage spread, the school days got longer and longer. I stayed to myself and just ignored what people said. I was finally taking Jesse's advice. I was ignoring everyone. I finally had that part of his advice down, or at least I thought I did. I obviously didn't. If I had really been successful in ignoring them, then the second part of Jesse's advice would not have been any problem at all. When you successfully ignore something or somebody, they don't bother you, they don't get to you. They were getting to me in a way I didn't think possible. I had always been so kind and compassionate, but now I felt something growing inside of me that I didn't think would ever be possible. It was hate. Pure, deep, and ugly hate.

Western Kentucky 1979

My junior year was nearly over when my sister returned to Maine, this time after filing for divorce, very pregnant and very alone. My heart was breaking for her, for all of us. This should be a wonderful exciting time. She was about to be a mother, Mom and Dad grandparents, my brother and I were soon to be an aunt and an uncle and all we could be was afraid. Nothing major had happened, but there was a cloud of fear hanging over us that reminded us that it could strike at any time.

I tried to stay busy. As the school year ended, I had a lot to do to get ready for my senior year. We were practicing basketball several days a week and I was looking at colleges. The one I had planned to attend was now out of the question. It was the school that had turned down my sister's request for admission the year before. The day her letter of rejection had arrived, I marked them off my list.

I decided on another university in Tennessee but I was ready to go almost anywhere, as long as it was away from home. I had to leave. My hate for everything I had known my entire life was growing. When some of our friends changed churches because of my sister's soon to be ex-husband and their unborn child, I could almost feel the hatred and anger bubble over inside of me.

Jesse cautioned me over and over. He saw the anger first. Others never saw it at all. I hid it well, behind self-righteous indignation. I told him I would leave as soon as I could. I would go to a Christian university where I could be spared from the hypocrisy, bigotry, and the downright hatred of these sinners. I couldn't wait to leave.

He would let me vent from time to time and quietly remind me that hatred was now living in me. That was something I simply didn't want to hear; and I honestly thought he had lost his mind. What did he know about what I was really feeling? It wasn't hate.

It was hurt.

I know now how right he had been. It took me many years to realize that unresolved hurt leads to hate, and unresolved hate … takes you a long way from home.

chapter 6

A Brand New Human Being

I continued to hide my true emotions from those who knew me best. I saw no reason to stoop to their level. They did not have to know that they were getting to me. I was becoming cold and distant, but the fear was another thing. There didn't seem to be a place deep enough for me to bury the fear.

Fear ruled my life back then. I had moments of complete terror. I wondered how long the Klan would hold back and what they would do once the baby was born. I didn't sleep unless I was exhausted and when I slept, nightmares would wake me. I began to have long talks with God trying to sort it all out.

When I first began to pray, I questioned God. How could people hate a helpless baby? Would the Klan try to hurt the child? I would have nightmares about lynchings and beatings. We had all read and seen what hatred could do.

As I prayed and begged God to protect this child, I finally came up with an idea. I got so much peace just thinking about it that I figured it must be from God. The answer was simple. The baby would be a girl. Even the Ku Klux Klan wouldn't hurt a little girl, especially a beautiful one. My sister and her ex-husband were both beautiful. I had seen mixed-race children on television and they were gorgeous even when their parents weren't. So, since my niece's parents were both gorgeous, she would be breathtaking.

I had lived long enough to see that even stupid, bigoted people were kind to the beautiful people of the world, especially beautiful women. The baby would be a girl. That was the answer. I became so convinced the baby was a girl, I asked Jesse what he thought a good name would be. I wondered if I should call or write my sister with my suggestions. He cautioned me about getting my hopes up, but I was certain that I was right. He would see.

As fall approached along with my sister's due date, my mother went to Maine to be at her side. Life continued as normal as possible. It was my senior year and we stayed busy. Basketball season was about to start and we had a new coach. The coach we loved and had all played for since the team began had to give up coaching us because of a new school regulation. He could no longer serve as head coach for both the boys and girls teams. They made him choose and he had been with the guys much longer. You could tell it was as hard for him as it was for us, but we were slowly making the adjustment.

Our practices were held in the morning. We had to share the gym with the boys' team. We would work out in the morning before class and they had the gym in the afternoon after school. The morning the baby was born, we were just wrapping up practice and hitting the line for our running drills. We normally ran till we were about to drop or puke, whichever came first. We trained tough, so there was no messing around or skipping out on the drills—no matter what.

We had finished about three drills and had three to go when I was called to the office. I remember so clearly picking up the phone and hearing my mom on the other end. I had not told her about my certainty that the baby would be a girl. I could hear the relief in her voice as she told me that my sister was fine and the baby was perfect. Mom was not expecting me to have anything but the normal reaction, when she told me: "It's a boy."

I can't remember if she told me his name, weight, or any of the details that usually accompany the announcement of a brand new human being. In my mind, all I could see was a picture I once saw of a black man hanging from a tree. I was terrified. I can't explain why that was my breaking point, but it was. I held it together for my mom's sake and quickly hung up the phone.

I was numb. I turned and left the office without a word. By the time I walked back to the gym, the team had already headed to the locker room. I was not thinking about the drills I had missed and headed that way as well. As I started down the locker room steps, I heard my name called from across the gymnasium.

My new coach had been waiting for me. "You're not finished," he said. I couldn't believe it. Everyone knew what was going on, it was clear I was upset, but he said it again, "You're not finished, get on the line." I gave him a look that had to say, "You have got to be kidding," but I walked to the line anyway.

He blew the whistle and I ran, down and back, down and back and by the third trip I was crying so hard I nearly fell on my face. I expected the whistle to blow any second followed by my coach berating me to pull myself together and finish my drills. Instead I heard my name called from the doorway. It was my old coach. He said, "I need to see her." He still trumped my new coach, so that was all that had to be said. As I looked across the gym, I saw the first look of real compassion and understanding I had seen in weeks. I still remember the concerned look on his face. Nothing more, just genuine concern.

I sat down in his office and cried. To this day I don't think the coach or anyone else realizes why the phone call from my mom hit me so hard. He never asked and it didn't seem to matter. He just said, "Stay in here as long as you need to." From that moment on, I knew I had a safe place at school.

I don't remember when I actually left the office. I didn't care. I barely remember changing out of my gym clothes, but at some point, I went to the main office, signed out and left. Jesse went with me.

jesse

chapter 7

Sunshine

Mom came home a few weeks later, with pictures! My nephew was so beautiful, just perfect. I was disappointed, but relieved they would not be coming home. They had decided to stay in Maine. They were safe there.

As the basketball season began and we started talking about the holidays, something completely unexpected happened. At least it was unexpected to me, but I think my mom knew it was coming. That's why she had such a tough time with the entire situation. She knew how her father (my grandfather) would react to his new great grandchild. My grandfather, Pa Pa to us, would not accept our family's newest addition.

We knew everything had changed as Thanksgiving approached. We always had a big gathering with relatives and friends. Many from my Mom's side of the family came to our house for the holiday. We had the perfect place, a farm out in the country and a big farmhouse that had been built by my father's father. Thanksgiving at our house had been a tradition for as long as I could remember, but not this year.

I remember how sad and lonely my mom looked. It made me sick to my stomach, and the hate and anger in me began to build again. It had subsided for a little while after the birth of my nephew, but now this was like gasoline on a hot ember. If I could have known then what I know now, maybe the hate and anger would not have been so deep and hard to overcome, but I had a problem seeing beyond the moment. It is something I struggled with for years to come. I wish I had known then what I know now because, as impossible as it seems, this whole broken mess with my mother's side of the family was reconciled within a few short years.

As I have written this story, I've left out most of the names intentionally to respect my family's privacy to some degree. Of course, those who know us, know well the names and places I have mentioned. I want to protect the part of this story that is theirs and theirs alone to tell, but I can't continue without telling you more about my grandmother. Her name was Sunshine.

I wanted to share her name with you because that is what my grandmother was, pure Sunshine. At her funeral, the minister said he never knew anyone that suited her name more than my grandmother had.

She and my grandfather would be over one hundred if they were alive today. They were from a generation that demanded a woman be in submission to her husband, no matter what. They were wonderful grandparents. Lives full of the silly little things grandparents do that make you chuckle when you are with them and ache for them when they are gone.

One of the silly things my grandparents did was send a birthday card to each of us every year signed, "Happy Birthday, Ma Ma and Pa Pa." Inside every card was a crisp one dollar bill. We always laughed, "What do they expect us to do with a dollar?" But looking back, it was simply what they could afford, and to this day the memory means the world to me.

As my nephew's first birthday approached, no one anticipated the receipt of a card from my grandparents. After everything that had happened, we considered they had disowned us. We didn't know what else to think. But as the week of his birthday approached, the card came with my grandmother's unmistakable handwriting on the envelope. We thought maybe my grandfather was getting used to the idea.

It was not until we opened the card that we fully understood. The card held the traditional crisp one dollar bill, but there was only one signature. "Happy Birthday, Ma Ma." With the simple signing of a card, Ma Ma had defied her husband and said loud and clear, "You are wrong." To this day, I know if it had it not been for my grandmother, our family would have been torn apart for good.

Instead, our family not only reconciled, but by the time of my grandfather's death, he and my sister were closer than ever. My mother told me just a day or two before he passed away, she walked into Pa Pa's hospital room and my sister was curled up sleeping beside him on his bed. The thought of that image takes my breath away; and it is an image we would never have known had it not been for my grandmother, Sunshine.

chapter 8

Western Kentucky 1980

The remainder of my senior year was less than memorable. All I could think about was leaving. We still had some great moments, but to those around me, I became cold and distant. Not with my family and a few of our close and trusted friends, but anyone on the outside. I went through the motions that were expected of me and nothing more. My parents had raised me to be respectful and I was, for the most part. As my disgust and hatred grew, I curled up more and more inside myself.

Jesse was the only one I confided in. I didn't trust anyone else. Sometimes I even shut him out. Especially when he did not tell me what I wanted to hear, which seemed to happen more and more. He could see the anger I was holding inside. He said it was like a disease. Over and over he advised me that the only way to really deal with what I was feeling was to face it and work through it.

I didn't appreciate his advice. It was the same as the advice he had given me when I was younger. "Don't let them get to you. Just walk away." He was still telling me it was up to me and I didn't agree. I had not caused any of this and it was not my responsibility to fix it.

It was much later that I finally realized what Jesse was trying to say. Even when we have been victimized or hurt, our reaction and what we learn from the experience is entirely up to us. As I reminisce, I can't help but think about all the time I could have saved if I had just stopped and listened. Really listened.

As graduation approached, we had a lot of special events leading up to our final days at the school where we had spent the last twelve years of our life. I barely remember the details. I have a vague memory of my blue cap and gown and posing for pictures with my teammates at the end of the ceremony. I honestly don't know why the memories from my last two years in high school are so limited. Jesse would probably say it was because I withdrew from everyone. Not physically, but emotionally. As hard as it was for me to admit, he would probably be right.

After graduation, I only needed to endure one more summer before I could leave. I had a part-time job at a fast food restaurant. It was my dad's idea. I had spent every other summer working on the farm and Dad thought I needed the experience of working for someone other than him before I left home.

Even with the part-time job, I still had time to do what teenagers do and I started hanging out more and more with one of my younger cousins. He and I grew up together. He is related to me on both my mom and dad's side of the family. He and his siblings are double cousins. His mother is my dad's sister, and his step-dad is my mom's brother. His father died in a construction accident when we were all very young and his mother remarried my uncle. So they were always around, almost like siblings rather than cousins.

We spent a lot of time going to movies, the ballpark, just being teenagers. I started feeling as though most of the trouble had blown over. Occasionally, someone would say something stupid, cruel, or just down-right mean, but incidents were becoming fewer and further between. Things were better, but Jesse still insisted I had to deal with my anger and I simply didn't agree. I saw no need to deal with something that I was not ready to let go of yet.

Summer was almost over. The local schools were already in session and I was set to leave for college within weeks. I could not wait. As my excitement increased I began to let my guard down as I anticipated a new start. One night my cousin and I went to town, I have no idea why. It may have been to see a movie or just hang out at the plaza. The only thing I truly remember about that night was an encounter with a local man who often dressed like a woman.

I bet you weren't expecting that, especially in a small, country community. The guy was well-known locally and he apparently knew a lot about my sister and her ex-husband, the father of my nephew. We were standing in line in a convenience store waiting to pay for our purchases. He seemed to be under the influence of something because the minute he spotted me, he loudly began to rant about how my sister needed to stay away from black men.

Many are surprised to hear that the bigotry my family dealt with was never exclusive to the white community. There was just as much opposition and sometimes even more from the black community. As the guy continued to shout, his temper seemed to rise. It was obvious we needed to leave. I could not believe the rage. It brought it all back and seemed to intensify the feelings I had about the entire situation—especially as I saw him pull a knife from his pocket as we headed out the door. It was funny though, this time I wasn't afraid. I was simply disgusted. I had come to re- alize what cowards many of those who spew hatred really were.

Later that night I sat and talked with Jesse. I knew what he was going to say. He reminded me again how I would eventually have to deal with the anger and hatred that had taken root in my heart. I was hoping that this last incident would prove once and for all, it was not my problem. I had said nothing to instigate the vile rant that had most recently crossed my path. Still, Jesse insisted I had a problem.

We talked a little longer, neither one of us making progress in winning over the other. I guess we left everything agreeing to dis- agree, but the disagreement had finally driven a wedge between us. We still talked. He was like a brother to me, but I was no longer listening to anything he said.

chapter 8   39

As I packed my car to leave, I had moments when my heart almost broke. I had to leave and knew I would, but I had always thought when I left for college it would be a tearful parting from those I had known, loved, and respected my entire life. The college was only two hours away, but until this moment, I had spent very little time away from the Kentucky countryside I had loved my entire life. It was a heartbreak that I had not expected. Instead of the bittersweet parting I had anticipated, it was regret I felt, as if I were leaving a precious friend that had betrayed me.

chapter 9

West Tennessee / Fall Semester 1980

Mom and I arrived at the college a little later than most of the new students. I had received a note with the name of my roommate, but with all that was happening at home, I did not reach out to her like most would do. I really didn't care. I did not intend to get close to anyone because I did not want to share with them the details of my life that had caused such turmoil back home, at least not for now.

Jesse and I had talked before I left. I told him of my plans to stay aloof and alone for now. I was not in the mood to do anything but put my head down and forget. Of course, he thought it was a bad idea and I had stopped arguing with him. I just listened. Actually, listening would mean I understood and might possibly agree with what he said, and I didn't. I let him talk and I simply ignored what he said. So, I suppose to say I listened would be a lie.

My mom and I found my dorm without too much difficulty and within a moment I had located my room and knocked on the door. My roommate opened the door and with a big smile invited us in.

As you read my story, you will see and understand I have two moments in my life that I am ashamed of. This was one. My new roommate was a sweet girl, my age, new at the college just like me. I am sure she was anxious about how she would get along with a roommate she had never met. She asked me a couple of basic introductory questions. I introduced my mom and she politely left us to move in and settle in.

After she left, I began to cry. My mother said, "It will be OKAY." I said nothing. My new roommate was black. My heart was so weary. I knew there was no way she would understand what our family had been through. No one around the region could. We knew of only one other mixed-race family. The problems we had seen came from both the black and white communities; and many of the black women I encountered had been some of the toughest to deal with. My concern over my new roommate had nothing to do with racism, but everything to do with race. I just didn't have the energy to deal with it any longer.

My mother and I went to the dean's office and there, through tears, we shared our story. The dean suggested I switch to a new roommate. Mom and I were afraid that would send the wrong message (as if switching to a private room would not seem odd), but that was the decision that was made. It still makes me sick to wonder how she felt coming back to the room and finding I was no longer there. What else could she think?

To this day I think God was giving me a short cut to work through my hurt and anger, and I took another road. I got to know my intended roommate later on. She was a sweet, forgiving young woman that I believe would have helped me heal, if I had given her the chance. I am thankful I was later given the chance to fully explain what had happened, but for a couple of years, she was simply left to wonder. She finally got the answers to her questions when I spoke to the student body on racism my sophomore year.

We were having problems with threats made to mixed race couples on campus and I asked for the opportunity to tell our story. Later, my "almost" roommate approached me and gave me a hug. I showed her a picture of my nephew and she told me he was beautiful.

Several years ago I heard Joyce Myers say, "Sometimes God will allow really good people to go through extraordinarily difficult things to show the rest of us how it is done." I believe the same can be said for the roommate I missed out on. She was so much better than me. Sometimes God will allow extraordinary people to cross our paths so we can see how life should be lived.

chapter 10

Slippery Slopes

Many parents send their kids to Christian colleges and universities to delay releasing their young to the wiles of the world. That may have been my parents' intention, but even in a Christian school, you can find and get into a lot of trouble. For many students, it becomes a game. My school, like all Christian schools, had rules that most college students would find impossible to follow. Rules that, when broken, would get you on probation and sometimes expelled.

I settled into a private dorm room and fully initiated my plan to be left alone. It worked as long as I stayed inside, but as I let down some of my barriers, things started to change. My friendships on campus started to grow, and my friendship with Jesse became less and less important to me, almost strained at times, but I stayed in touch.

As I got to know others on campus, I did take the time to share with Jesse the feeling of acceptance I was starting to feel. He had been with me through so many down times and I wanted him to know that I was OKAY. Surprisingly, I was almost popular. This was an absolutely foreign experience for someone like me. I had endured bullying and harassment my entire life. The whole concept of inclusion had seemed unobtainable.

At first, I tried to follow the rules. I was actually very committed to being the model Christian student and an example to those around me. I was convinced that our Christian campus would be a religious utopian experience. It was a place where those of us who were worthy could commune with God and look down from our lofty perch at those who did not live up to our standards. We would show them how God intended for the elect to conduct themselves.

About two weeks after I began life as a coed, I began to slip from my lofty perch. It started when I accidentally overslept and missed our Sunday morning worship services. You have to understand how significant this was for me. Growing up, we never missed worship. If the doors were open, my parents insisted we attend. My parents were leaders in our church. They both taught Bible classes. My dad was one of the primary people called on to fill in for the preacher from time to time and he led the singing services once a month.

Dad taught the teen class on a regular basis, and we hosted parties and bonfires for the youth group several times a year. Attending services on Sunday morning and Sunday night was something we did without thought. Missing was out of the question. We never missed Wednesday night Bible studies either. During the summer we would have special services and seminars that would sometimes bring our congregation together for seven nights in a row. To miss worship services without illness or emergency, especially something as sacred as the Sunday service, was heresy to me.

The morning I missed my first Sunday service, I called my mother crying. Looking back I think my reaction was not for the one missed service. It was the understanding that I had just stuck my toe across the line of a very slippery slope.

As I continued down the slippery slope of rule-breaking at my school, the one thing that saved me from expulsion was my gift for "spin." I could have easily been a politician. I was a master at saying what had to be said while keeping back the details that would end my college career. I was very sneaky, but I also think getting kicked out of school was simply not in God's plan for me.

God, in spite of my stupidity, spared me the humiliation of being expelled or worse.

My slippery slope in college eventually became a slide into the abyss as I continued to test the waters. I quickly saw what happens when you break the first rule. When you take the first drink you swore you would never take or you cross the line you drew in the sand of your life, things change quickly. It becomes easier and easier to cross that line the next time, then the next and the next. Soon, you no longer remember where you drew the line in the first place.

The most bizarre thing about my behavior was that it was an absolute, polar opposite to the kid I was back home. I had been the model Christian teen. I did everything my parents and my congregation asked of me. In high school, if you had told me the things I would do once I left home, I would have called you a liar. Yet, within one to two years of high school graduation, I had broken every rule I had ever been given. Keep in mind that I am not talking about the rules applying to major crimes, though I most certainly could have been convicted of a misdemeanor from time to time. I don't think anyone in my life felt the need to reiterate those rules outside of the original Ten Commandments; and I think that may have been part of the problem. The rules I broke are far too often discounted as "sowing a few wild oats." Unfortunately, all crops, even the wild oats we have sown, eventually have to be harvested.

chapter 11

Radio! Let the Games Begin!

In spite of my spiritual downfall I did actually find the path to my professional future. Most religious institutions of higher education have some type of assembly. Our version was called chapel, our daily time of reflection, worship, and campus announcements.

One morning, during my first semester, an announcement was made concerning the campus radio station. They needed students to read the news. Before this time, a career in broadcasting had never occurred to me. This is a fact that really steams some of my co-workers today. Many in the broadcast industry have dreamed since childhood of one day being on the airwaves. For me it was a whim.

As I sat and listened to the announcement, I remembered our local radio station broadcasting our basketball games back home. When the sportscasters would interview us about the big game, they said they liked talking to me. They had told me many times, they liked the way I sounded on the air. At the time I just assumed it was because I was a public speaker and competed in speech competitions for the school's Future Farmer's chapter. I was never nervous and thought no more of being on the radio than I did sitting across the table and talking with a friend. It had never entered my mind again until that moment.

So as the announcement was made, I thought, why not? If they liked the way I sounded back home, maybe I could pull it off here; and I needed something to do other than study. I bored easily and needed a new distraction. After chapel, I went straight to the radio station. It was love the first time I opened a microphone. I had found my destiny or at least a part of it. I am not sure my parents liked the idea. The prospect of my major changing from education to broadcasting seemed ridiculous at first. With all we had been through over the last few years, once they got used to the idea, they were just excited to see me excited.

I had not talked to Jesse for over a month, but I had to fill him in. Too much was changing; and he deserved to hear it from me. At first, I felt guilty. It had been so long since I had touched base with such a dear friend, but Jesse never seemed to mind. I think I could have avoided him for months at a time, and he would always act as if we had just spoken the day before.

He was thrilled that I had found some direction and thought I was on the right track. It felt right; and I wondered why I had never considered broadcasting before. My greatest dream had been to follow in the steps of Tanya Tucker. Every country girl that could carry a tune longed to be the next teen star. Now that I was older, I knew music was a childhood fantasy, but broadcasting would let me touch the edge of the industry. Over the years, I have found many frustrated musicians in broadcasting, especially in Tennessee. It is a natural transition for star-struck egomaniacs!

West Tennessee Spring Semester 1981

Changing my major changed my associations on campus as well. I found myself hanging out with a new set of friends. Some were a little more spiritually sincere than my old friends. Many were politically motivated, but most, like me, were just trying to fully partake of the college experience. Have fun, learn a little, and since we were at a Christian school, don't get kicked out.

We worked for hours putting together shows and news presentations. Of course we thought they were brilliant and our friends would lie and tell us they really enjoyed them. We spent weekends sneaking into dance clubs. A fake I.D. was not the issue. In the early eighties, very few clubs carded. This was still back in the day. If you sneaked into a club and did something stupid (and you were underage), you were liable for your own actions. Society still believed in personal responsibility.

Our biggest concern was covering up our campus parking stickers so that someone driving through the parking lot would not notice our cars. If someone from school saw a car where it should not be, they would take down the license number and turn us in. Yes, we had professors that spent their weekends trying to catch students at places where they were not supposed to be. Not getting caught was our game, catching us was theirs. Hiding the campus-parking sticker was as easy trick. We would peel the backing off of the edges of a larger sticker and use it to cover our campus sticker. Then we would simply pull it off without damaging the school sticker and return to campus.

Monday mornings were spent huddled in whispered conversations about the weekend exploits. Who got caught, what was their defense, and would it hold up when challenged in the Dean's office. It seemed every weekend, especially during the spring semester, ended with disciplinary actions being taken against someone on campus.

The end of my freshman year came way too quickly. I was having way too much fun, or at least I thought I was. The week before finals I realized I had not spoken with Jesse since early in the semester. I could not believe it had been that long. I could not go home without filling him in. So much had happened.

As usual, Jesse acted as though we had spoken just yesterday. We talked for hours and, inevitably, we ended up talking about things I didn't want to talk about. I think that was why I "forgot" to touch base with him for months at a time. I reflect on those times and I know Jesse would agree. I spent a lot of time like an ostrich with my head in the sand, refusing to deal with what was going on around me.

Jesse reminded me, I was in the middle of doing things that I had promised myself I would never do. Now I was making excuses. I made excuses for my actions and my inactions. Insisting I didn't care, when he and I both knew I cared more now than I ever had.

I told Jesse I would be home at the end of the next week and we could talk more then. I assured him that I would be careful and I would try to get some sleep. Sleep was something I thought was simply an option. I prided myself on staying up for two and three days at a time. Working multiple shifts at the radio station, studying all night to get through a class, then pouring back enough caffeine to wake an army. Everyone around me was concerned. They cautioned me over and over that I was moving at a pace that was going to catch up to me sooner or later. I didn't agree. They were right. I was wrong.

chapter 12

Splash Down

Final exam week was crazy. Everyone's schedule was changing and we needed a lot of extra help at the radio station. None of my tests were scheduled at convenient times to accommodate sleep and what I needed to do at work. Of course, sleep was still an option, so I didn't bother with it.

I worked every shift I could on the air, studied all night, took my tests, and got maybe an hour of sleep before doing it all again. This went on for three days. Finally, my tests were over. We had reduced the hours of the campus radio station to the less-demanding summer schedule. Hardly any students were on campus, and our broadcast license allowed us to reduce our hours of operation during the break. I had packed and loaded my car before my last test, so I was ready to leave campus any time.

I had made arrangements with friends a couple of days earlier. One of our cohorts lived nearby and had left the day before. The rest of us were heading out together. We were planning on crashing at our friend's house for one last night. We would sleep in and have breakfast together the next morning before parting for summer break. We left campus late and no one thought to call ahead to make sure the plans had not changed. By the time we reached our destination it was after campus curfew, and our friend had arrived home sick with the flu. Her mom had not known she had an entourage following her home.

We obviously had to change our plans. Several lived nearby and decided to head home. A few drove back to campus with plans to call the dorm supervisor. We were locked out so the only way back on campus was to get her out of bed and explain what had happened. We knew she would be upset. I was not sure what to do. I lived a little further than some of my friends. I still had an hour and a half to travel across two-lane country roads to get home, but I didn't want to go back to school. The dorm supervisor was looking for any excuse to write me up. I thought my friends would fare better facing her without me.

I finally came to the only solution that made sense. I would get some coffee and hit the road. I laughed when I thought how surprised my parents would be to wake up tomorrow morning and find me asleep in my room upstairs.

Telling my friend's good-bye, I reassured them I would be fine. A little coffee or maybe a lot of coffee, but in less than a two-hour drive I would be home and asleep in no time. As I pulled out of my friend's driveway and started looking for an all night convenience store, I remembered Jesse cautioning me about taking stupid chances. I laughed and thought he would probably think this was one of those times. They were all just paranoid, Jesse and my friends. I knew my limits. I felt great. I didn't even feel sleepy, but decided to go ahead and load up on coffee.

The drive home was a long drawn-out trail. The trip took me through several small towns past a lot of farmland and many areas where the roadway was surrounded by woodlands. Not the types of scenery conducive to helping someone stay alert, especially at one o'clock in the morning. I was having a tough time staying awake and I realized I had to pull over. I decided to stop in a little town near the Tennessee-Kentucky border. It had a small town square with a few stores and a bank. I pulled into the bank parking lot and fell asleep almost before I put the car in park.

I am not sure how long I slept. I never looked at the clock again until much later. The only thing I remember clearly was waking up and remembering I had pulled over to sleep in the bank parking lot and I had to get going. I am not sure why I woke up with the urgency to leave, but I remember clearly thinking, I have to go, Mom and Dad will be worried. Isn't it funny? I was so concerned with worrying my folks. They thought I was safely tucked away in my dorm room, still on campus. Surprise!

The last thing I remember was pulling out of the bank parking lot. I literally remember nothing past putting the car in gear and hitting the gas. I was completely unaware of anything that transpired until several miles away I awoke as my car left the roadway. I remember waking up as the car began to bump along the grassy roadside. That was just in time to feel the impact from hitting a mailbox post made from a railroad crosstie. I felt as though the car would never stop rolling down a hill, and finally it splashed into a pond.

It was one of those dream-like moments where you wake up and shake your head and wait for your mind to clear, hoping that what you just witnessed was only a dream. It took a minute for everything to sink in. I started realizing my predicament was real as the water poured into the car. I wasn't submerged yet, but I knew I could be quickly. I had no idea how deep the pond was. We had two ponds on our farm that were deep enough to submerge a tractor. I decided I should probably get out of the car.

Every time I tell this story, someone asks if I was afraid of drowning. Honestly, when I saw the water, I knew I was OKAY. I was as comfortable in the water as I was on land. I have always been a strong swimmer and at the time was a lifeguard. I knew I would be safe, once I realized I was dealing with water. I was not concerned about being trapped because I was moving and had everything from my dorm room in my car. I knew, if I had to, I could find something to break a window. Fortunately though, back in the day, we had this old-fashioned thing called a window crank; and with a few turns of the handle the window came down and I bailed out.

As I slunk out of the muddy pond (and it was mostly mud), I began to realize what had happened. I remembered the bank parking lot and I shook my head in disbelief when I realized I had sped off concerned that Mom and Dad would be worried. They didn't even know I was on my way home. I was going to surprise them. "Surprise, Mom! Surprise, Dad! I am somewhere in the woods. My car is in a pond. The front end is smashed from the crosstie I encountered before hitting the water. For the record, the next time you want to set a mailbox post, a crosstie is a good choice. It didn't budge one inch from the impact. Surprise!"

I walked back up to the road and there was no one in sight. I was in fact on someone's farm. There was a farmhouse across the field on the other side of the road. By this time it had to be two or three o'clock in the morning. This was long before the cell phone. My only hope of getting any assistance was for a kind soul to happen along the roadway in the middle of the night or to walk through the field and knock on the door of the farmhouse.

As I walked up the driveway, I rehearsed what I was going to say. I knew the odds were in my favor that I would find someone cautious, but helpful. I also knew there were some farmers who would not look kindly on someone strolling up to their door in the middle of the night. There was also a possibility that someone would meet me at the door holding a shotgun and would simply shout for me to leave before they proved they had a shotgun. I said a little prayer and knocked on the door.

I had to knock several times before I heard any movement inside. I still had no idea what time it was. After a couple of minutes of cautious questions through the closed door, the occupants opened the door just enough to take my parents' phone number. They agreed to a make the call and handed me the receiver just as the phone began to ring. I stood there dripping wet and covered in mud on their porch. The phone rang and rang as though no one was home, until I finally heard my half-awake mother on the other end. "Mom…" I said. "Surprise!"

It took my parents about an hour to get to the wreck scene. By the time they pulled up we were experiencing what Francis Scott

Key described as "dawn's early light." They pulled in just ahead of a wrecker. My dad had called a friend with a rig to meet him along the roadway and together they found my pitiful little car, headlights still glowing just under the water. My mom jumped out of the car crying and hugging me. I felt so bad. She was so upset. I don't think I have ever felt so stupid in my entire life. I could not believe what I had done. I had plenty of time to think about it while I was sitting on the roadside waiting for my parents to arrive.

As they pulled my car from the muck and mud and the water spilled out from under the doors, I began to take a survey of what I had ruined in my little dive. My stereo and record albums, all of the posters I had collected for my dorm room. A life-size poster of the Bee Gees had not only adorned my dorm room wall, but had a place of honor in my room back in Kentucky as well. That wall was going to look so empty. All of my clothes were covered in mud. The luggage they were packed in was ruined, of course, but the clothes would wash. I was taking a mental inventory as my mother was giving voice to my thoughts.

By the time the car was loaded onto the wrecker, my mom's relief that I had survived the crash was quickly being replaced with questions. Frustrated questions every teen hears when they do something so remarkably stupid. "What were you thinking?" tops the list. Of course, the obvious answer to that question is one you only come to in hindsight. If I had stopped to really think it through, none of this would have happened.

Mercifully, my parents took me home and let me go to bed. I am not sure if I slept for a few hours or a few days. I only remember waking up and it was already the heat of the day. I went outside and opened the door to my ruined car. Mud covered everything. I started to pull a few things out of the car and set them in the shade to wash and try to salvage. After a couple of trips back and forth to the car, I stopped and walked around to the front. My dad had talked on the way home about the dent in the front of the car. It was from the impact of the crosstie I hit before I went into the pond. Curious about the damage, I wanted to check it out for myself. I had not thought of it until that moment. The dent should be right about the same place as the "N" that had been scratched in the hood of my car since high school. I guess I was hoping the dent had destroyed the letter. It hadn't. It was still there.

I talked to Jesse later that night and after the expected, "What were you thinking?" we talked about that "N." I told him how happy I was to be rid of that car. That was a lie though. I loved that car. Still, I was glad I would no longer pause when my hand would pass over the letter as I washed the hood. I would no longer find myself staring at it as I visited with friends in the school parking lot. No one at college had ever noticed it. The car was white. Unless you knew it was there you didn't see it; but once you saw it, you could see nothing else.

Now, it didn't matter. It was gone. It was over. I could move on. Jesse didn't say he agreed with that last part, and even if he had, I would have known he didn't mean it. He was glad I would not have the constant reminder, but he also knew, as I did, this journey was far from over.

chapter 13

Western Tennessee
The College Years 1981 – 1983

By the second half of my sophomore year, I was a radio veteran, or at least I thought so. I was the student news director. I had the ability to rip and read even the toughest news copy, no matter how many foreign, multi-syllable names were included. The campus program director had given me a partial broadcast scholarship declaring that I was a natural. I was happy, sort of.

There were still underlying problems. Instead of dealing with them, I worked very hard to ignore them. I ignored the pain, the hurt, and most importantly, the hate I carried for what I had once treasured back home. Ignoring it was a lot easier, or at least I thought so at the time. The problem with ignoring something so big is that eventually, when your mind is at rest and you find yourself alone, it is the only company you have.

My years in college were unfortunately pretty typical. Dreams of a career I had no concept of how to begin. Time spent in required classes that seemed pointless and often were. Weekends making excuses to stay on campus and not deal with questions I didn't want to answer or face back home. Staying out late, then sleeping in until hunger pulled me out of the dorm. Skipping any semblance of responsibility in favor of self-indulgence.

I had a romance here and there, but nothing that felt real. I don't think anything in my life began to feel real until I hit rock bottom. That came the summer between my junior and senior years.

It seemed like everyone I knew had a story to tell. They all had stories about their many exploits, especially with the opposite sex and the excitement of living on the edge. I didn't get it. I had lived on the edge of the edge and it had only left me feeling empty.

Still, I began to push the edge even further, thinking I would be a rock star to everyone I knew. The stories I would tell. As I became more and more the person I swore I would never be, a funny thing happened. Everyone I knew began to pull away. It was as if they could sense I was getting in too deep. The realization finally hit me, but it was already too late. The stories they bragged about were nothing more than a lie. It was a lie none of them ever intended to live, and that they quickly ran from when it got too close.

I found myself understanding for the first time how my sister felt at seventeen—when after a deceitful first marriage, it seemed as though she had ruined her life before it had even begun. I truly thought I had ruined everything. I had no idea what to do next. I could not wrap my mind around just starting over and climbing out of the pit I had dug around my life. Running away seemed so much easier.

I could not face those I had known for the last three years in college. I left and never went back. I gave no explanation and I doubted that they would care, so I never gave them the chance. The jolt from hitting rock bottom had awakened something buried so deep inside me. I thought it could never shake lose. The hate Jesse had warned me about was still there and I was finally seeing the damage it had done deep in my soul. I simply stopped caring.

Common sense should have told me that now was the time to reconnect with my childhood friend. It was no surprise that we had lost touch in the last few months. At the very least, he would make me feel better. He always did. But this time, I could not face him. I couldn't face him anymore than I could face myself.

I didn't like anything. I wore hate on my face, in my attitude, and in my faith. My faith had taken a real beating. I had always had doubts and now it seemed impossible. Nothing I prayed for came through. It was as if God were mocking me. Everything I wanted seemed out of reach. I spent night after night locked in my room until I had thoroughly locked myself away, not only in a room, but deep inside the bitter and hateful person I had allowed myself to become.

chapter 14

Nashville Tennessee
Fall Semester 1983

It is amazing to me that God doesn't wash His hands of us sometimes. Thinking back, I wonder what He could have possibly seen in me to give me a second chance. It amazes me even more how He uses those around us to get our attention from time to time.

The things I remember most about hitting rock bottom is how long I allowed myself to stay there and the friend that finally told me to get up and get moving. No, it wasn't Jesse. He was still reaching out to me even though I had completely shut him out. I made every excuse I could think of not to talk to him. I avoided everyone I could, but there were a few people in my life, whether I wanted them there or not.

When I mentioned earlier running away, I didn't say where I ran to. After a brief stop in Kentucky, I headed to Nashville. I had always wanted to go. Ever since I was a kid, I had dreamed of a music career in the Music City. The university I had originally planned on attending was there. Now it was my only real option. There was no way I was going back to West Tennessee. Not only could I not face them for all I had done, but I didn't want anyone to see me either. In my self-loathing state I had stopped caring about everything, including my diet and exercise. My weight was at an all-time high. I was miserable.

When I transferred to Nashville to finish school, I stayed in a private room but still had to deal with suite mates—girls who shared a common area with me in my dorm. Unlike my school in West Tennessee, these girls had attitudes. They didn't pull any punches, and if you were being stupid, they told you so.

I tried hard to keep them at arm's length by sharing some of my exploits, hoping they would see I was trouble and just leave me alone. Instead, after a particularly long dissertation of my life and how lousy it had been, one of the girls rolled her eyes and said, "If I had to be around you all the time, I would stay depressed." Funny thing though, she didn't leave. She made the statement and then changed the subject to something a little less dramatic and not about me. I was stunned. I don't think anyone had ever told me so clearly and so bluntly that I was no fun. I guess I knew it, but hearing it so clearly was like a wake-up call.

That night, I finally got up the nerve to talk to Jesse. He was the only one who knew me well enough to sort this out. I would not have blamed him if he had completely ignored me as I had him. As usual, it was as though we had talked just the day before. Our first conversation after so many months was short, but it was a start. I had to deal with the hate I had buried so deeply and the only way to begin was to just begin, and Jesse had been there from the start.

It wasn't long until Jesse and I were talking almost daily again. I was finally listening to what he had to say. I was convinced that I was growing and finally getting past the hate and hurt. He was not convinced. It was not that simple, he said. For awhile I listened, but as I started to get excited about life again, the walls to all the things I didn't want to deal with went back up.

I got involved with campus activities, started making friends, losing weight, and quickly became restless with campus life. I had an opportunity to move off campus and I jumped at it. The rent for the apartment was no more than my dorm fees, so my mom agreed to the change. I assured her that I could finish school and would even start looking for a job.

I vividly remember flipping through the yellow pages my first week off campus. It seemed to make sense. I had experience in radio, so look for a radio job. It never occurred to me that I might not be qualified to work in a broadcast market the size of Nashville with only college experience under my belt. It is a good thing too, or I might have talked myself out of trying.

The first station I saw was a legendary AM station with a history dating back to the early days of radio. Of course, I did not realize any of that as I looked through the phone book. They were just the biggest ad I found, so I assumed they were a big deal. Why not start at the top? I called and surprisingly got an interview. The supervisor in charge of hiring was a bit of a flirt and I didn't see any reason not to play along. What could it hurt? As it turns out, I got the job. My boss was a flirt, but harmless; and I began my broadcast career in Nashville, Tennessee at the age of just twenty-one.

I was a producer for weekend shows and quickly caught on to the routine of the job. I still look back to those early days amazed at the opportunity. I worked with legends in the industry. One gentleman had been in radio since it began and told stories about a huge recording artist routinely stopping by to pitch a song. That was back in the day when a bottle of whisky went a long way in helping a new artist get airplay.

Not surprisingly, life off campus was not helpful in my desire to complete my college degree. I quickly lost all interest in finishing school even though I was just a few hours away from graduating. I was starting to have too much fun again or what I thought was fun at the time. I was working in the industry I was studying to join, so the decision to drop out and go to work full time was an easy one.

chapter 15

Music City

Jesse was unhappy with my decision to leave school. He was not surprised, but hated the idea of me leaving something else in my life unfinished. He continued to remind me of the issues I needed to confront. Deep down I knew he was right, but for some reason I just couldn't let it go. It still hurt.

For the first year I stayed busy. With the excitement of my new job, I barely thought about all the things Jesse insisted I needed to resolve. Constant activity provided the noise I needed to shove it all aside once again.

After the excitement began to fade, the routine of radio was setting in. With boredom, the clouds began to roll back across my mood. Eventually, even the busiest mind must rest, and you again find yourself alone with an unwanted guest.

I was doing well, even making a name for myself, in a city I had dreamed of as a child. Granted, in my childhood dreams I was singing at the Grand Ole Opry, but it was still Nashville. The problems began when I started working the night shift and began spending too much time alone. I worked while most slept and slept while most worked. I asked for any and all the hours I could. I still have check stubs with ridiculous weekly hour totals.

Broadcasting has never been great complying with labor laws, especially back in the day, and who would complain? Most of us loved it; and if we weren't willing to work crazy long hours, there were plenty of people waiting in line to get their chance on the airways. Radio became my enabler. They would allow me to work as many hours as I could stand, and I didn't have to spend time thinking about caring.

In my early years in radio, I did it all. I was a reporter and a disc jockey, I did commercial production work, answered phones, filed reports, swept the floors. You name it; I did it. I loved it and I loved being busy. Part of my job description was to be the air talent for remotes when we would broadcast live from an event or business around town. I was already spending a lot of my spare time at clubs, but as work took me to more and more of the hot night spots, I found myself in clubs several nights a week.

If I was working, there was always something to do. It was when I was on my own that I seemed to have a problem knowing what to do with myself. It seemed I was always on the hunt for someone, anyone. I hated being alone, but I usually regretted the short dysfunctional relationships I had. No one to write home about, for sure; but I continued to hope and look. Unfortunately, where I was looking seemed to be, as the song says, "in all the wrong places."

I mentioned earlier in my story that I am absolutely ashamed of two things I have done. You heard one. Now it's time to share the other.

I was out one night. It could have been Monday, Thursday, or Friday, who knows? Going to a club was never limited to any specific day of the week. I remember it was a club on the southeast side of town. It was a "yuppie bar." If you don't remember what a "yuppie bar" was or what the term means, it was a place for young upwardly mobile professional, or young urban professionals, Google it if you want to know more. Yuppie was a slang term from the 1980s.

I never seemed to have a hard time meeting guys. I just never met really great guys. They were always out of work musicians (and in Nashville there were a lot of those), or they were drifters with a slight alcohol or drug addiction. Every now and then I would meet a guy that seemed a little too good to be true. They seemed nice. Some were even employed. Occasionally they were even tall, which was an issue since I am just over six feet tall myself. We would meet and I would think for a brief moment that maybe... just maybe he had promise. Then I would hear... the rest of the story within a day or so.

I spotted this guy from across the dance floor and he spotted me. Tall, cute, and dressed as though he was employed. We hit it off immediately and danced and talked for hours. Late in the evening, he told me something that should have sent me out the door, but it didn't. He told me he was married. To this day I don't know why I thought he must have meant that he was married and getting a divorce or separated. I suppose I never dreamed anyone who was married would be out dancing in a club.

Looking back, it makes me sick. I knew better, but I liked the guy and I didn't want to think about the reality that he had just shared. I agreed to see him again. So, I shoved everything I had ever been taught into the pit in my soul, where I hid so much more. I was so lonely that I could not bring myself to say no.

Fortunately, my conscience got the best of me; and the relationship, if you can even call it that, was very brief but the damage had been done. I grieved over that relationship. Not the loss of it, but that it had ever occurred at all. The shame I felt was like a white-hot pain. As if I had turned the tables on the God I once thought was mocking me, and now I was mocking Him.

jesse

chapter 16

A Warm Welcome?

With even more to lock away and bury deep inside myself, my life became a whirlwind. I jumped from one bad relationship to another. I covered my lonely moments with whatever was available to blur my thoughts. I worked to exist. Not really moving forward or backward. Just existing.

Over the course of my first three years in Nashville, I moved into an apartment with a friend from college and another girl I had befriended in a bar a few months earlier. One is still a close friend to this day. We all seemed to be on the same page. Get by, have fun, meet guys. That was our lives in a nutshell. Not much depth to any of it, but we thought we were having fun, sowing a few wild oats.

My roommate from my college had the same spiritual background as I did, but she didn't seem to have the same questions. She lived more at peace with herself and God. Me, my mind was consumed with guilt and doubt. Guilt over all I had done that I knew was wrong and doubt that God was real at all.

This was another period in my life when Jesse was not around, not that he had not tried to reach out, but I was at a place of such shame and doubt that I could not face him. I guess I was jealous of his strength and certainty that everything would work out and that God was always with us.

I doubted everything. How could anyone be sure? I had grown up in the sixties and seventies. Everything was questioned, especially God. So many questions had been raised as we learned more about the age of the earth. None of it correlated with what I had been taught in Bible School. I had a fascination with archaeology and geology; and it raised more questions than answers as to who we are and where we came from. I had doubts and questions that consumed my mind and eventually ate away at my heart.

This was about the same time period that I met a local preacher. He was from the same tribe of Christians I had worshiped with my entire life. He recorded a weekly radio broadcast sermon. I was the production engineer in charge of getting it all done. Every week I would sit and listen as he spoke. He struck a familiar chord with me and I began to miss the fellowship and peace that I felt during worship time. I began to think that all the doubts I was having about God were because of the absence of church in my life.

On several occasions the preacher asked me to join his congregation for worship. I always declined, but one night I wrapped up work a little early. It was a Wednesday night, so I decided to go to the mid-week service. The church building was located in the same neighborhood as the yuppie bar I mentioned earlier. I arrived a bit late so was unable to speak to the preacher till after the service had ended.

I decided to wait around to say hello and give the obligatory, "Great job" and pat on the back I had been taught preachers like to receive after a pulpit performance. As I waited in line, I noticed no one was really speaking to me. That was unusual. Churches in the "Bible Belt" take pride in singling out their guests. They make sure everyone leaves with a few religious tracts in hand and the understanding that they have to come again. Otherwise, they will be hunted down by the eldership for an explanation as to why they are "forsaking the assembly." None of that was happening this time. They seemed to be keeping their distance.

When my turn came with the preacher, I said the usual, "Great to see you, good lesson…" to which my friend said, almost too politely, "Well, thank you for coming." And then, clearing his throat to make sure everyone heard what he said next, he continued. "And the next time you come, please dress more appropriately."

You see, I had made the monumental mistake of going straight to the church service from work. Broadcasting, especially radio broadcasting, has never had much of a dress code. If anything, we were required to look a little edgy. People were disappointed if we looked normal, so I was wearing a black leather jacket and faded jeans. My hair was a bit wild as well. It was the style; and I never thought for a moment that anyone would find my appearance inappropriate.

I was speechless. I could not believe it. Everyone around him stood looking at me as if I were an unruly student and the teacher had just reprimanded me for something I had done. I am not sure… but I bet I smirked. I probably rolled my eyes too, because in that brief moment the preacher had reinforced everything I thought and felt about "the faithful."

From that moment on, I never gave church another thought. I went with my parents back in Kentucky; but even then, I didn't want to be there. I was there for them. I didn't want to hurt them, and I didn't want them to worry about me. This was a journey I had to take alone.

chapter 17

A Man Named Bubba

I spent the next summer in a haze of parties and bad relationships. My roommates and I got along great. We partied together when we weren't working and became closer with every stupid mistake we made. We were kindred spirits I suppose. One of the girls actually ran a club we frequented. It was a country bar with cowboys, rednecks, and two-stepping. We would spend time there till she closed and sometimes all ride home together.

One summer night my roommate from college and I decided to stop by the club for just a moment to say "Hi." Our other roommate was working and we were not in a mood to party. Unusual I know, but we were getting older (or at least we guessed that was the issue). Neither of us could really explain it, but we were both getting sick of men. At least we were sick of the type of men we had been dating. We agreed we were just going to run in, say "Hi," and then maybe catch a movie.

Everything changed the minute we walked into the club and caught sight of what was on the dance floor. There in the middle of the room towering over everyone else was a strapping hunk of manhood. I believe Ellie Mae Clampett would have referred to him as a very "pretty man"!

My roommate says she spotted him first. She may have, but honestly, I think it was a draw. He was hard to miss. Suddenly our plans for a movie changed. We had to check this out. A very tall, very pretty, and apparently very single newbie was at the club. He was definitely new. A guy like this you don't forget.

We immediately sought out our roommate and proceeded to interrogate her for information on this guy. She didn't have a clue. The club was packed and she was behind the bar mixing drinks because a bartender had stood her up. I am not sure when he spotted me, but he did. I was one of the few women in the bar that could look straight at his chin. Eye to eye was out of the question, even for me. He was over six and a half feet tall, six feet eight to be exact.

I'm not the shy type, well actually I am in many ways, but back in the day, at least with guys, I wasn't. There was only one problem. I thought he was completely out of my league; so I looked, but steered clear.

From time to time, I would look at him and he would look at me as if we were having a conversation across the dance floor. About an hour had passed when I noticed the mystery man walking toward my table. He was being led by another man that I had noticed at the club from time to time, but we had never met. Unlike the mystery man, he was a typical "Tennessee Bar Fly." Long hair, bushy beard, blue jeans, a faded shirt, and a cigarette perched on his lips.

I quickly realized the guy leading the charge was named Bubba. I swear that was his name. This is another one of those moments in the story that you simply have to know the name to get the full effect. Bubba introduced himself and then explained he had been watching us. Once he saw neither of us was willing to make the first move he decided we had to meet. He confessed that he didn't know either one of us, but thought we were perfect for each other and someone had to point out the obvious.

After asking our names, Bubba made the introductions. Then with classic redneck flair, he encouraged us to "get to know each other" and left us to do just that. What followed was a moment of uncertain, awkward conversation; then I began to interrogate my mystery date. I was not going to let this guy pull me in. I had to find out what was wrong with him, because there had to be something wrong with him. With guys like this there always was.

First, I wanted to know who all his dance partners had been and there had been many. Including one moment when I counted at least five dancing with him all at the same time. As it turns out, they were friends of his new neighbor; and they were just being neighborly, showing him around town. He had just moved to Tennessee from up north.

Secondly, and rather obvious, was his place of origin. His accent gave away the northern part, but I had no idea what he meant when he said he was a Yooper. I later discovered that was a nickname given to those who were born in the Upper Peninsula of Michigan, the area of wilderness just north of Wisconsin and just south of Lake Superior. He was practically a foreigner.

As the night continued, so did the questions. I wanted to know everything. I was certain there had to be something wrong with this guy. I was not going to let myself get caught up in another dead-end relationship. Finally, after seeing I was not going to let down my guard, he excused himself and went back to his harem on the dance floor.

My roommates immediately swooped in for all the details. They were not pleased to see I was steering clear. At least my roommate running the bar wasn't pleased. The other one, who was still insisting she saw him first, was now thinking it was her turn to check him out.

From that moment on I tried to ignore him, but it was a small club with an even smaller dance floor; and he towered over everyone there. You could not look up without spotting him, dancing, having fun, and now ignoring me.

With the "pretty man" now dancing with every girl in the bar, I was thoroughly convinced that I had been right. He was simply out of my league. I decided to leave. As I was heading for the door, something stopped me. I can't explain it, but I felt like I had to tell him good-bye. Against my better judgment, I decided to wait a few minutes before leaving—at least until the song ended. If he didn't come off the dance floor, I would go ahead and leave.

As the song ended, he headed off the floor and spotted me near the exit. He smiled and waved. At first I thought he was just waving good-bye, then he headed my way. As he got closer, I realized this guy was huge. I had not stood next to him. When Bubba introduced us I was sitting down. I stayed on my bar stool through my entire interrogation. Now standing next to him, staring right into his chin, I saw just how big he was. I also noticed the visual, up-close evidence of him being the recent college football player he claimed to be. This guy was in amazing shape. I know he realized I noticed from that smug little smile he had on his face as I stood there gawking at him.

I stammered for a minute and then told him it had been nice to meet him and hoped he enjoyed Nashville. I reminded him that we might see each other from time to time, especially if he came back to the club. He knew from our earlier conversation that I was a regular and the club's manager was one of my roommates. Instead of just saying bye he asked for my number. A little floored and caught off guard, I stammered, but gave him my business card. As I handed it to him, he asked if he could call me for a tour of Nashville the next weekend. Before I could say yes or no or before I remembered I had to work nights the next weekend, I nodded yes and quickly headed for the door

chapter 18

It's a Start…

Amazingly, I never gave the encounter another thought. I had given my number to enough guys to know they never call. By Thursday, I had locked in my schedule and knew it was going to be a long weekend at work. I was working the overnight shift every evening and I was going in early to cover for a co-worker who had to leave by ten both nights. No fun for me this weekend. I had resolved to make the best of it when my phone rang. It was the guy.

Immediately I realized I had blown it. I had told him I could show him around town and now I was going to have to stand him up. He actually seemed disappointed that I had to work, so I suggested he let my roommates show him around. He agreed and I gave him directions to the apartment.

As soon as we hung up from the call, I started regretting what I had done. What if he really did like me? What if he ended up liking one of my roommates more? What was I thinking? It was too late now, so I decided to not let it bug me. I was good at covering up my feelings, I could lock this up too. No one would know I really liked this guy. No way was I going to let myself get hurt again. Let him trample one of my roommate's hearts instead. Then I would help her get over him and congratulate myself for not letting him get to me.

Friday night at work was…Friday night at work. The usual crazy phone calls followed by nearly falling asleep at three in the morning. Getting through an all-nighter meant being so jacked up on caffeine by the time my relief arrived there was no way I was going home and going to bed. I walked into the apartment and noticed it was empty. Not a good sign. I wondered where my roommates were; and I was really hoping one of them was not with the guy.

I sat back, turned on the television, and was just settling in with a bag of popcorn to watch a movie. That was when I finally noticed the light flashing on the answering machine. The first message was the guy. He was saying he could not find the apartment and needed better directions. The message ended and the next one began. This time he sounded frustrated. He said he had been driving around in circles for an hour and he was going home. The next message was one of my roommates telling me not to worry. She was crashing at a friend's house and would be home in time to wake me up for work.

Grinning to myself, I decided I was sleepy, crashing actually. The caffeine was wearing off and my mood had suddenly changed. Maybe I still had a chance with the guy. I was going to sleep well, maybe even have a nice dream. I had not forgotten how to dream and something told me that things might be different this time.

When I worked all weekend and worked the night shift, my day began about the same time as my roommates. The one that ran the bar was on pretty much the same schedule as I was. The other was an accountant, but usually stayed out late on the weekends and rarely got up any earlier than we did.

About three in the afternoon we were all awake and ready to hear the details of the night before. If I had been working, I always had a great story or two. The people who call radio stations in the overnight hours are highly entertaining. Of course, the bar always had a skirmish or two but the most fun came when our roommate that had a real job shared her exploits. She seemed to attract every dysfunctional guy in town and never had a problem putting them in their place. It was always fun hearing the recap.

The most surprising part of the review was that no one had seen the guy. When he had not shown up, they left and never thought another thing about it. They assumed he would come looking for them at the bar. He never showed. I told them about the voice mails, and we all agreed we would probably never see him again. We had barely finished our conversation when the phone rang. It was the guy and he wanted to talk to me.

I think my heart was racing as I took the phone. I really liked this guy and he seemed to like me. It was a little weird that he was calling me. I had a few boyfriends, but I had to do the pursuing. I would call them and set up a time for us to see each other. I often paid my own way. Never had a guy like this one given me any attention.

Trying to be cool, I waited a second before saying hello. He wanted to know if I was busy Sunday evening. He still wanted that tour. I explained I would have to get some sleep after working the overnight shift again and then I could meet him somewhere about six. He said, "Well, if you will give me better directions, I can come and pick you up." I laughed and agreed and went over the directions to the apartment one more time.

jesse

chapter 19

The Grand Tour

That night was the longest air shift of my life. The night dragged by. I got home and tried to sleep, but was having no luck. I finally dozed off out of pure exhaustion. My alarm clock rang at five and I started getting ready. My excitement had worn off. I was convinced that he would not show, but thought I would go ahead and get ready. If he didn't show up, I had some shopping I needed to do.

My roommates were both at home when the doorbell rang at five minutes before six. There was no way that would be him. It was probably a neighbor stopping by to hang out. A few of our neighbors were guys our age, actually a little younger, all still in college. They liked coming over because we had furniture.

One of my roommates yelled for them to come in and then stammered and said, "Well, hi. You are not who I thought you were." Our visitor said, "Who were you expecting?" I was still in the back bedroom, but I could hear the "Yankee" brogue and knew it was the guy.

"We thought you were one of the neighborhood bums." My roommates laughed. "It's about time for them to show up." "Sorry to disappoint you," I heard him add. "No disappointment here," they said, "but we were betting you wouldn't show."

I decided I had better get out there before they made a mess of things. I quickly shut up my roommates and pulled my date from the apartment, saying we had to get going. He immediately laughed and wanted to know why I was in such a hurry. "Do the streets in Nashville roll up on Sunday night?" "No, but my room-mates can ruin a good thing before it starts." I answered. I guess he was not sure how to respond and instead smiled, opened the truck door, and said, "OKAY, let's go."

"Where to?" he asked pulling out of the parking lot. I had not really thought about it. This was not a date I thought would ever happen. I was completely unprepared, but quickly decided down-town would be a good place to start. He was driving a company truck and explained exactly what he did for a living as we headed to the interstate.

He had been transferred to Nashville from Michigan as an in-spector for a roofing manufacturing plant. He traveled across the region inspecting roof installations and issuing warranties. It was not his dream job, but it was a job until he got a call from the State Highway Patrol in Michigan. He had graduated with a criminal justice degree and was planning a career in law enforcement. He was just working for the roofing company until they had an open-ing for him in the academy.

I told him I was a little surprised they had a waiting list for the police academy. He quickly added that they didn't unless you were Caucasian and male. He immediately saw me bristle at what he had said and wanted to know why. I got defensive and told him, "That just sounded a little bigoted." It was his turn to bristle. "I am just stating a fact." He said defensively, "One of my best friends and roommates in college was a black guy. One of the best guys I know." He added. "I'm not a bigot."

I apologized and told him a little about my nephew. I explained I was a little sensitive. "Sensitive?" he questioned. "I think you are a little more than sensitive." He added. "Do you walk off balance?" I wasn't sure what he meant, so he continued. "You're not just sen-sitive, that's a pretty big chip you are carrying around on your shoulder." He teased, "I bet you walk a little crooked carrying something that big around." I thought, Jesse is going to love this guy, but I was not ready to have this conversation. Instead, I changed the subject and pointed out the Nashville skyline as I gave him directions to Nashville's famous Music Row.

We drove past the radio station, some of the recording studios, and then looped around to catch a glimpse of Vanderbilt University. Five minutes later, we were driving past the Mother Church of Country Music, more commonly known as the original home of the Grand Ole Opry, the Ryman Auditorium. He could not believe I had never been. I told him that I had never had the chance. I would never admit that I had dreamed for so long of singing on that stage that I couldn't stand the thought of being there in the audience. It was a childhood dream I just couldn't let go; and I knew going to a show would make me want it even more.

We made a quick pass by the downtown honky-tonks and Printer's Alley then headed back out to the interstate. He was amazed at how small the city really was. Nashville is a town you expect to be as big as its reputation. If you consider all of the suburbs, it is much larger than it seems, but you get a small town, country feel less than a mile outside of downtown.

"What's next?" he asked heading out of town. "We can go by the mall." I suggested. He liked the idea and followed my directions to a mall on the east side. Since it was Sunday, the mall had closed early. We spent the rest of the evening driving through the area checking out a few key landmarks and grabbing a bite to eat. We had a great time talking. Just getting to know each other, as Bubba had suggested we do the night we met.

We ended our evening early. We both had long weeks ahead of us and I was going to start it tired. I had worked extra hours covering the weekend shifts. My primary job was a split shift as the radio station's traffic reporter, so I had a very early morning ahead of me. He had to drive to a job site four hours from Nashville the next morning, so he planned to be up early as well.

We said goodnight and he promised to call me when he got back to town later in the week. He offered to walk me to the door, but I was afraid he would want to come in, and I had no idea who was lurking inside. Much to my surprise the apartment was empty and that was fine with me. I did not care where everyone had gone. I was tired. I had an early morning and a very long day ahead of me; and I think I had some pretty sweet dreams coming my way as well. I slept like a rock that night and, yes, the dreams were nice too. I couldn't help but wonder if the pretty man was having the same dreams as me.

chapter 20

Catching Up

It was a crazy week. A week that would make you think you were living in a much bigger city with the way traffic was moving, or I should say, not moving. By mid-week, we had already dealt with three overturned tractor-trailers and one had been carrying cattle. The Nashville police force had to play cowboy rounding up the misplaced animals through the inner city neighborhoods. It was absolutely hysterical listening to the chaos over the police scanner.

By Thursday, I was convinced I would not hear from the new guy again. I relived every moment. I convinced myself that I had blown it when I called him a bigot as the night had begun. Then I rationalized, he had gone through with the entire evening, so it must not have upset him too much. If he had been upset, wouldn't he have taken me home right away? Then I remembered that he was the one who suggested we end the night a bit early. Who knows, I thought, and who cares? I did. I cared. I finally admitted. I cared and I was afraid I already cared too much. That never seemed to work out for me.

By Friday night I had not heard from him and had resolved I wouldn't. At least, I had not fallen too hard. I went out with my roommate, but I was not in the mood to do anything. I would rather sulk at the apartment and go to bed early. I left the club and chastised myself for caring. I was angry that my weekend off was a bust. I had turned down extra work thinking I would have plans and now nothing.

I was just about to go to sleep when the phone rang. It was him. He said he was sorry he had not called earlier. He had stayed out of town and would not be coming home till the next weekend. He was leaving the job site he had been working with all week and was heading to another site the next day. His work schedule had unexpectedly gotten crazy. Everyone needed everything done at the same time and he was the only inspector in the area.

I didn't want to admit how relieved I was, but I was. I was disappointed he would be away all week, but at least he had called and that was something. We talked for an hour. He had an expense account; and the company he worked for was picking up the call. After we said goodnight, I realized I had not asked where he was or where he was headed. I don't suppose it mattered. When you travel for work, one city looks like the next. One of my roommates was an accountant and traveled all the time. She had told me she could sometimes forget which city she was in, if she had had a busy month on the road.

She also told us about all the guys she met while traveling. I got a little jealous as I began to wonder if he had forgotten to call or was he just too busy with someone he had met on the road. Putting that thought aside, I decided to focus on the positive. He had called and we had made plans for the very next weekend. I couldn't wait.

After the long week I had been through, the weekend was even longer. The new guy was out of town. I wasn't on the work schedule; and I had no interest in hanging out at the club with my friends. So, Saturday night I decided it was time to talk to Jesse. It had been almost a year this time. I couldn't believe how quickly time slipped away. I wondered if he would ever get tired of my neglect and finally just wash his hands of me? I should have known better after so many years, because, as usual, Jesse acted as though we talked every day.

I talked non-stop about the guy. I think I practically gushed. I even mentioned praying that God would let this one work out. I was so tired of being alone, and even though I had relationships over the years, I never felt anything but alone. None of them made me feel like they cared, only that I was simply convenient. If I were really honest though, with a couple of them, they had cared, but it was me that found them convenient. Never had the feelings been mutual. If they cared, I didn't and if I cared, they didn't. So, like I said, I had never felt anything but lonely, and I was tired of lonely.

Jesse and I talked most of the night. I couldn't sleep, and sometimes I didn't think he ever did. He always seemed to be sitting and waiting for me anytime I wanted to talk, as if his world revolved around mine. I am not sure why I took such a friend for granted. I told him every detail and I knew he was happy for me. All he had ever wanted was for me to be happy.

Saying goodnight to Jesse this time felt different. As if I would not lose track again; and maybe I wouldn't. Who knows, maybe I was ready to work through some old wounds. A hot, new boyfriend would make me consider it, but I didn't want to read too much into it yet. We were really just friends, for now. Maybe that was all he was looking for, a friend. After all, he talked a lot about going back to Michigan. If the academy called, I had no doubt that he would leave immediately. For now, I decided not to worry about it and to pray the academy stayed over-crowded and unwilling to take on new cadets for at least a few months.

chapter 21

Highs and Lows

Tuesday night I had barely walked through the apartment door and the phone was ringing. It was my guy. I could hear people in the background, so I assumed he was at dinner and just using the pay phone. "Where are you?" I asked. I was surprised when the name he mentioned was one I recognized. It was the name of a boy I had gone to high school with and I told him so. He said, "Yeah, I know… same guy."

At first I thought I must have misunderstood him. I said, "I went to school with a guy that had that same name." I continued, "He has a brother and sister and the whole family lives across the field from my mom and dad." "I know." He said again, "It's the same guy. As a matter of fact, I can see your parents' farm right now."

I couldn't believe it. What were the odds? I thought. "Crazy, isn't it?" he continued. "Oh, and they say 'Hi.'" As he finished, I heard my old school mates yelling "hello" in the background. I had forgotten they ran a roofing company. They were hosting my guy as the new inspector from a roofing manufacturing company they used.

We talked for few minutes before he said goodnight. It was suppertime and everyone was ready to leave. He was trying catfish for the first time. I had to laugh, he didn't sound excited. "Aren't they bottom feeders?" he asked. "Yes, but if you bread them and fry them, who can tell?" I teased him. "Can't wait," he said sarcastically. "I will see you this weekend." He added, "We're still on aren't we?' I assured him we were and said goodnight. The phone practically floated back onto the cradle. I was hooked. I had to talk to Jesse.

Jesse and I talked every night that week. I was nervous. I had never felt this way about anyone. I rationalized there had to be something to this guy. Otherwise, why did he show up back home, right across from my parents? I thought that must be a sign. I wondered aloud to Jesse. "Do you think he saw the gravel roads I ran a thousand times? I can't imagine him being back there." I knew it was a silly question, but it seemed so strange. I started reminiscing about home and, before I knew it, I was talking about things I had not thought about in years. Jesse was glad. It was time, he encouraged. Maybe he was right.

That weekend was probably the best weekend of my life. I had the weekend off again. I would miss the extra cash on my check, but it was worth it. After all, my guy was paying. That was so foreign to me. Everyone I had ever dated always managed to get me to pay part of our bill for dinner, a movie, or whatever we decided to do. I had seen every trick in the book when it came to stiffing a date for the bill. My dates always seemed to manage a trip to the restroom just as the bar tab or the dinner bill arrived. With someone else picking up the tab, I could stand missing a few extra work hours.

We spent the entire weekend together. I was on a cloud by the time he left Sunday night. He had to go out of town again and would be away for two weeks. He was actually flying this time and I would get to see him off at the airport the next morning. The new airport had just opened and he was on one of the first flights. Our radio station was broadcasting live for the grand opening, so I was going to be out there working anyway.

The next morning I had already finished my work when my guy's plane was scheduled to leave. I stuck around to say goodbye. We had a little extra time and spent it talking as we waited for the plane. I still think back on that conversation and wondered what in the world I was thinking. I have the uncanny knack for asking questions that some might never think of, often causing myself unnecessary trouble for bringing something up that should have been left alone.

I guess I was running out of things to say, and instead of just staying quiet, I asked, "So, do you ever meet anyone when you are out of town?" He laughed and said, "Well yeah, I meet a lot of people." "You know what I mean," I added. "Do you meet women… women you date?" I finished, immediately wishing I could pull every word back in my mouth as I said it.

"Yeah…" he said. "I do." Then he continued and I began to feel sick. "I really like you, but I mean, we just started seeing each other…" He paused and then continued. "You don't expect me to stop seeing other people, do you?" The way he said it was almost as if he couldn't believe I would even suggest such a thing. "No, of course not," I said, trying to sound like I didn't care and knowing I was blowing it. "I was just wondering and feeling a little jealous about who you will spend time with next weekend."

He laughed and said, "Well, to be honest with you, I have been in this city before and there is someone I see when I am there." I was crushed. I obviously felt more for him than he did for me. I am not sure what I said at that point. They called for his gate and we said goodbye, a little awkwardly. As he walked away, he didn't look back. I blew it, I thought, I really blew it. I wanted to cry, but refused to allow myself to care. Taking a deep breath, I headed for the parking lot and went back to the station. I had work to do or, at least, I was sure I could find some. I did not want to think right now.

jesse

chapter 22

Old Flames

I could not believe how quickly things could change. As elated as I had felt Sunday night, I had never felt lower than I did just twenty-four hours later. I wanted to talk to Jesse. I knew he would listen and he did. He listened while I cried and talked about everything I was feeling from caring way too much, way too quickly for a guy I barely knew, to the old feelings that were surfacing as I began to allow myself to feel again. It was a rough week.

The phone never rang. As the weekend approached I was sick wondering about this other woman. Was she prettier than me, or worse, was she thinner? Nothing robbed my security like a thin rival. I could be twice as pretty, but always felt inferior to a thin and stylish woman. I still felt like the awkward, too tall, too fat adolescent that had been bullied every day by my classmates.

I decided to call an old boyfriend to distract me over the weekend. I had hoped to work, but I was getting way too many hours during the week and the boss insisted he could not allow me to work so much overtime. Reluctantly, I gave in and worked to track down my old friend.

He was typical of the guys I had dated since arriving in Nashville. He was a borderline bum. A really nice guy, but he drank too much and never seemed to take responsibility for anything. He was an only child with wealthy parents and spent most of his employed hours driving tour buses for bands.

I lucked out. He was in town and looked forward to seeing me. Of course, I would have to come to him. Forget coming by and picking me up. Since I was coming over, he asked me to pick up a twelve pack. Big surprise. By the time I arrived, the party was well underway. There was always a party at this guy's house. Everyone was already drunk or high and thrilled to see me. Everyone wondered where I had been, but quickly lost interest when I started to tell them.

As the night wore on, I decided to spend the night. Everyone else was staying and I was in no mood to be alone. I don't think I closed my eyes. Nothing felt right. As soon as the sun was up, I said goodbye and headed home. I knew when I left, I wouldn't see any of them again, and I was relieved. I was finally growing up or maybe I was just waking up.

I did not hear from my northern friend for three weeks. I was thoroughly convinced I had freaked him out by being too clingy, too quickly. Jesse and I were back to talking every day. He was helping me work it out. He was so relieved to hear I had seen the last of some of my old friends, and he listened as I continued to peel back layers of anger and hurt that I had buried deeply for too many years. It was funny how feeling anything reminds you of other feelings you don't always want to feel.

Amazingly, three weeks to the day after we had said goodbye at the airport, the phone rang. It was the guy. We talked a little awkwardly at first, but soon we were laughing and making plans to see each other the next weekend. I was flying high again, but determined not to blow it this time. I was afraid I was driving Jesse crazy. My emotions had been like a roller coaster these past few months, but he didn't care. Like always he was there and just listened.

Friday night, right on time, my guy arrived at my door. After a few moments of harassment from my roommates (whom I had threatened with a fate worse than death if they said anything about how upset I had been over the last few weeks), we quickly left. He suggested we catch a movie. It was as if nothing had changed. We were getting along just like we were the Sunday night before our awkward parting at the airport.

I still have no idea what movie we saw. I was way too distracted. After the movie, we went to supper and the moment I had been dreading began. He wanted to talk about what had happened. He apologized for not calling, but he didn't want to lead me on. That statement was exactly what I was hoping I would not hear. He obviously didn't feel as I did, and now he was saying it.

The woman he had seen while he was away was not the problem. He began to explain how he intended to eventually go back to Michigan. I told him I understood that when the academy called, he would have to leave. That was not it, he said. The academy had made it pretty clear that he should not expect to hear from them for at least a year maybe two. I didn't understand at first then I saw it in his eyes. There was someone else, someone special back in Michigan.

When he had been transferred to Tennessee, they had broken up. He had asked her to come with him. They were engaged, but she refused. He was convinced, if he gave her time, she would come to her senses and see they were meant to be together. He really loved her. I could tell and it broke my heart.

As broken-hearted as I was, I couldn't be mad. He had never been anything but honest with me. We continued to see each other, but things had changed. We both seemed to pull back the minute we noticed we were getting too close.

As usual, I worked as much as possible and tried really hard not to care, but I couldn't help it. For the first time since I had been in high school, I didn't bury my feelings. Jesse was there and I was glad. I don't know what I would have done if he hadn't been. I needed someone to talk to.

My roommates were no help. They begged me to dump him, "Don't let him keep stringing you along," they insisted. I could not make them understand that you can't string someone along when you have been completely honest with them. "We're just friends," I told them. "Just keep telling yourself that till you believe it," they said. I knew they were right. To him, we were friends. To me, we were so much more, and I could not understand why he couldn't see it.

As Christmas approached, I had a feeling things were about to change and it was a change I was not looking forward to. I knew he would be traveling back to Michigan, not just to see his family, but for his company's Christmas party. The company he worked for was in the same city as his ex-fiancée. He had called her and they were planning on seeing each other as soon as he got to town. He was excited and I tried to be excited for him, but I couldn't. I knew something he had not yet realized. We were meant to be together; and I was not going to stop praying for him to see it too.

The company wanted him to drive up for the Christmas party. They wanted to inspect the truck to make sure it was holding up with his intense travel schedule. He would arrive just in time for the company party; then he could continue north to see his family for Christmas. I know his plan was to spend a little time with his ex-fiancée, hoping they would reconcile and he could convince her to travel north with him for the holiday.

That was a rough Christmas. I had a hard time sleeping the night of the company party. I imagined all sorts of scenarios and I did not like any of them. I stayed a few nights with my family in Kentucky over Christmas and spent most of the time clinging to a stuffed bear he had given me that fall. I was sick. My poor parents didn't know what to do. My mom had seen my heart broken so many times that she had learned to just leave me alone. She knew I would talk to Jesse if I really needed to talk. So she didn't worry (or at least she tried not to), but moms know daughters better than they know themselves. It just takes the daughter awhile to realize it.

I had to get back to Nashville right after Christmas. The radio station was sponsoring a big New Year's Eve event, and I was one of the hosts. I was still unloading my car when I saw his truck pull in the parking lot of my apartment complex. I was floored. I didn't know he was back and now here he was. I stopped and waited for him to park and climb out of the truck. He helped me carry the rest of my bags up the stairs to the apartment and gave me a hug once we got inside.

My roommates were out so we had the place to ourselves. We just chatted at first. I guess it was what you would call small talk. After a few minutes, I couldn't stand it any longer. "What happened?" I finally asked. He just smiled and shook his head. "It's over," he said. "I'm sorry," I told him. We both knew I was lying.

"Her dad is mad at her," he added. Then he began to talk and didn't stop until he had told me everything. He told me how he had met her his senior year in college. She was a bartender at a club that he worked in as a bouncer. She was divorced and was not ready for another relationship, but her family had talked her into it. They really liked him, especially her dad, but it was not enough. They were through, he said three or four times before moving on to stories about his family and Christmas back home.

"Then all through Christmas, instead of being upset over her, all I could think about was you," he said reaching into his coat pocket. "I got you something." It was a music box. "I like the song," he said, handing me a little acrylic piano with a wind up key sticking out of the side.

He had already wound it up and turned it on as he sat it in my hand. I immediately recognized the song. It was one of those songs that, to a disc jockey, was like nails across a chalkboard. It was in the same category as the seventies hit, "Feelings… whoa whoa whoa feelings." But as every note played and the familiar Carpenter's tune ran through my mind, we both had tears in our eyes as we sang along to "We've only just begun." "Why don't we see where this goes?" he said, as the music box ran down. I could not have agreed more.

chapter 23

Happy New Year

New Year's Eve had just gotten very exciting. Instead of my roommate joining me, I now had a date. The year before, my college friend and now one of my current roommates, had taken my extra ticket. We were the belles of the ball. As much fun as we had the year before, I knew this year was going to be the best. Nothing could compare to the feeling that you were spending time with someone you might be with for a lifetime. From the moment we decided to "see where this goes," we were all in. We went from friends to so much more within seconds. Our New Year's date was just the warm-up.

We transitioned quickly into a very committed couple. We were talking marriage within weeks. Just four weeks after he had returned from Michigan, he asked me to marry him. It wasn't a formal proposal. As a matter of fact, his supervisor was in town and was upstairs in the townhouse my guy rented. We had just had supper and were headed out to the boat show at the convention center. We were downstairs loading the dishwasher. Suddenly, he stopped what he was doing gave me a big hug and said, "When are you going to marry me?" I said, "When you ask me." He said, "I'm asking." To which I said, "Sure."

Honestly, I wasn't sure he was serious until I heard him tell his boss. "We just got engaged." His boss laughed at first then said, "Are you serious?" We both nodded and he said, "Well, congratulations… let's go to the boat show." And we did.

From that moment on, we started making plans. It became a little more official the morning he drove me to work. The roads were icy and he had a little more experience on ice than I did. He actually laughed at the way we freaked out over a little bit of sleet in the South. Actually, he didn't just laugh at us. He mocked us!

The minute we walked into the studio my co-workers began to interrogate him. They were typical morning guys, silly and mouthy, good as gold, but sometimes a little overbearing. They cornered him, shined a light in his face and asked him, "What are your intentions? She is like a little sister to us, you know?" These were the same guys that shot bottle rockets at me across the studio and loved to moon me from time to time. I quickly shoved him back into the hall and sent him on his way, but the interrogation continued. Now all of Nashville knew I was getting engaged. I still didn't have a ring, so it wasn't officially official, yet.

After work that morning, my co-workers turned more serious and actually wanted real details. One of the guys had only been married a short time and highly recommended making the commitment. He even gave me the address of a chapel we could use for the wedding. It was nearby and he suggested we check it out soon before it was booked up for the year. The other, a little less committed to anything, cautioned me not move to fast. That advice was constantly ringing in my ears, because Jesse had said the same thing. But I knew this was it or at least I hoped so.

My future husband was Catholic, so it was decided that his family would be more comfortable in a more formal setting rather than a small southern church. The chapel my friend had mentioned sounded perfect. It was within walking distance of Music Row. My office was less than a mile away, so it was easy to check it out. We fell in love with it before we even went inside. The chapel is on one of Nashville's many college campuses. Nashville's nickname, "Athens of the South," is not from the replica of the Parthenon at Centennial Park. The name was given to the city for its wealth of colleges and the Parthenon was constructed in recognition of that honor.

Wightman's Chapel is situated on a side street near Vanderbilt University. Part of the Scarritt-Bennett Campus, the chapel was becoming the most popular place for weddings in Nashville. Surprisingly, the date we wanted in the fall was still open. On our first visit, we paid the deposit and spent the rest of the afternoon walking through the grounds and planning our big day.

I had a hard time convincing my fiancé that I didn't care what my ring looked like or how big the stone would be. I was not a jewelry person. I wanted a ring, but could not have cared less about the details. I was easy to please and didn't need a fancy or expensive ring. We found a jeweler that worked out of his basement; and he had a beautiful ring he had bought in an estate sale. He suggested we use the diamond from the ring and let him craft a new setting. I loved the idea, the ring had history and, more importantly, it was cheap.

Much like the actual proposal, the night my future husband slipped the ring on my finger was a little odd. The gentleman that had made the ring, along with his very sweet wife, wanted to watch the official proposal and we didn't have the heart to disappoint them. So on a ratty sofa in their basement my "pretty man," got down on one knee and asked me again to be his wife. We have Polaroids to prove it. Of course, I said yes.

chapter 24

The North Meets the South

The next obstacle was the dress. I am just over six feet tall. I had lost weight and was thin enough to wear dresses off the rack, but they were inches too short. My mother and I went from shop to shop, always with the same results. Frustrated, I hired a seamstress and my ivory wedding dress was handmade.

We had the dress, the date, the chapel, and the ring—now all we needed was the family. I don't think either of us had any idea what a challenge bringing our families together would be. I can safely say that this is another moment in my life that, in hindsight, I can easily say, "What were we thinking?"

If we had stopped to think it through, the potential conflicts would have been obvious. He was Polish Catholic from way up North. So far up North, to go any further would make you Canadian. My family had been in Kentucky for as long as any of us could remember. Our state couldn't really claim the South, since we had remained neutral in the Civil War. We were a farming family and still are. Sharing a border with Tennessee, we were thought more often to be hillbillies than Southern.

My family had been in America so long we had lost track of our roots. We were simply, "All-American Mutts" and proud of it. Some in the family had tracked one branch of our family tree back to the Revolutionary War. I had several cousins that had talked of joining the Daughters of the American Revolution, an organization that I know very little about and had a feeling would bore me to tears. I was drawn to the more colorful branch of our family's tree that had ties to a couple of Irish bootleggers.

It was a completely different ancestral story than the one presented by my future husband's family. His grandfather arrived on Ellis Island from Bohemia as a little boy. His grandmother was from Austria and the entire family had an ethnic, old-world, feel that I had only read about. His grandfather had earned his living as a music teacher and bandleader. It was a polka band called "The Merry Makers." The majority of the band members were part of the family. They played weddings, picnics, and parties and were often the featured entertainment at the town's band shell.

Our favorite foods were pork barbecue and catfish. My fiancé's family was more accustomed to pierogies and smelt. The notion of having a wedding without a party was also unheard of to my future in-laws. They wanted a band and plenty of food and drinks. My family's idea of a wedding was a traditional, Southern, church wedding. Just like the one my sister had back in the seventies. Followed by a cake, punch, and peanut reception and, of course, butter mints were added for a formal affair.

My future sister-in-law was a baker. She planned to arrive early in the week to make the wedding cake. My fiancé insisted that she wanted to do it. I wasn't so sure. I could only imagine the stress of traveling across the country with a family in tow and having to make a wedding cake at the end of the journey. I was hoping I was not starting out with one big strike against me in the eyes of my future sister-in-law. It sounded like way too big of a job to accomplish while on a road trip.

Her daughter was also the flower girl and she was a bridesmaid. I couldn't imagine making a small birthday cake, much less the cake she was planning, especially in the middle of all of the normal wedding activity. I questioned my future husband again and again, but the answer was always the same. "Really, she wants to do it."

As the wedding day neared, Jesse and I were talking more and more. My old insecurities were resurfacing. I was starting to think about how quickly we had decided to marry so soon after my fiancé's final breakup with his ex-fiancée. I was starting to think maybe he was settling for me. He was from a big family. It was no secret he wanted to be married. Was I the consolation bride?

Jesse listened intently, never reminding me of his recommendation that we move a little slower and more cautiously. I always felt better once I talked it through, but the wedding date was inching closer; and I had a sinking feeling my fiancé might back out all together.

The week of the wedding was like the end of a pilgrimage for my future Northern relatives. They had driven over seven hundred miles. It's a journey that takes at least twelve hours and could take as many as fifteen or sixteen hours. It all depends on how many whining passengers you have in the car and how many stops you are forced to make. My future husband handed out maps and a schedule as everyone arrived. The rehearsal was Friday night followed by the rehearsal dinner at a local restaurant. The wedding was on Saturday afternoon; and we needed everyone there for pictures two hours early. Otherwise, they were free to check out Nashville. That is, everyone was free, except my future sister-in-law. She had a cake to make.

Glad to have one less thing to think about, I left the cake completely up to them. I had a chapel to decorate. My parents had helped with much of the wedding cost, but never thought spending "good money" to rent a chapel was necessary, so we had covered that cost ourselves. We were on a budget, trying to save as much money as possible for our honeymoon in the Smokey Mountains. I decided to decorate the chapel myself, borrowing ferns and props from a friend who coordinated weddings. She offered to help, but I wanted to do it myself. If the truth is told, I had a hard time accepting help from anyone. The walls I had built long ago were rock solid. I didn't trust anyone and didn't like to count on anyone but myself.

As I busied myself every waking minute with last minute wedding plans, my fiancé was occupied with his family. They seemed to get lost going across the street for a newspaper. We were frustrated, stressed out, and had not had a moment alone in days. My future husband rented a townhouse about thirty minutes from Nashville. I decided to drive out, hoping we could steal a moment to ourselves. I had forgotten his place was "wedding cake central."

I walked in just as the drama began. His sister had made several layers of cake and had spread them out in the spare bedroom to cool. The townhouse was to be our home after the wedding and my very large, very annoying cat had already taken up residence. With the cake cooling in the upstairs room, no one gave the animal a second thought… until they went to retrieve the cakes.

The cat had started nibbling and by the time they interrupted his feast, he had made a general mess of the entire situation. At this point, I could not have cared less if there was a big wedding, much less a cake. Jumping in the car and eloping was sounding better all the time. I quickly saw I was not helping, so after a peck on the cheek from my future husband, I drove back into town.

I was off work the week before the wedding, but I went to the radio station anyway. It was, after all, my home away from home. I was met in the hallway by one of my co-workers and close friends. As soon as I saw him, I unloaded. I told him everything. I ranted for ten minutes, finishing with details of the ruined wedding cake and the declaration, "I don't want to know how they fix it." I think I cried a little and even laughed over the cake, but the end result was an opportunity to vent to a friend, instead of unloading on the people I would soon call family.

I relived the entire mess later that night as I updated Jesse on the day's events. The chaos was not helping to calm my fears. The wedding was just two days away, and I still didn't feel like any of it was really going to take place. There was a little voice inside of me that doubted that my fiancé loved me and doubted that his family even liked me. This was the first time I had met his family and nothing had gone right since they got to Tennessee.

Talking it out helped. I was hoping I would be able to sleep and finally told Jesse goodnight. My family was arriving the next day and I was wide awake, imagining the fireworks when the two families met. My future mother-in-law had insisted there be a wedding party. A real Polish-style wedding celebration. The quiet little reception we had planned would not do.

My parents knew there was a second reception being planned for the "Yankee" side of the family. I am not sure how they felt about it. Mercifully, they stayed quiet and made their plans to attend the reception at the chapel. They had volunteered to stay and clean up after the wedding was over, making sure all the props and tuxedos were returned and everything was put back in pre-wedding order.

I have no real idea what my future in-laws thought either. I imagine they thought my family was ridiculous for not attending the later reception. Unless you grew up in the "Bible Belt" it was hard to understand. My parents were members of a very conservative church. Almost everyone we knew was a teetotaler. They steered clear of any alcohol and had never set foot in a bar. We were on such a tight budget that the only logical place to hold the party was the bar and club managed by one of my roommates. She was opening early so we could celebrate before the normal Saturday night crowd hit the dance floor. There was no way my family could attend. No one back home would understand. We all seemed to agree to disagree by staying silent and made plans to celebrate in our own way.

I imagined all sorts of confrontations when everyone finally met face to face for the first time. That moment was getting closer by the second and I needed sleep. I finally turned off the lights, closed my eyes, and surprisingly slept.

chapter 24   109

chapter 25

Wightman Chapel

Surprised and relieved that I was able to sleep through the night, I got up early and went to the chapel to start setting up. My family would be there by the afternoon, just in time for the rehearsal. My sister and her husband were coming and so was my nephew. He had just turned nine years old and was getting cuter every day. My brother and sister were part of the wedding party along with all my fiancé's siblings. This was turning into a major production.

The best man for our wedding was an old friend of my future husband. They had worked together in Michigan. He assured me over and over that he would get the groom to the chapel on time. I told him the time was not my concern. Just make sure he shows up. No one but Jesse knew how concerned I was about being left at the altar. Things had moved so quickly that I couldn't blame him if he got cold feet. Jesse reassured me that he would be there keeping an eye on things. He would do all he could to make sure the day was perfect.

At the rehearsal, things seemed to drag on for hours. We finished late and were dealing with a lot of grumpy people looking forward to being fed. We finally sent everyone to the restaurant and it seemed as though we were going to get a moment to relax. I was looking forward to sitting down, having a nice meal, and really getting to know each other. Yeah, right. I had barely walked into the restaurant when we received a phone call. It was my future brother-in-law, (I won't say which one) and he was lost. He had no idea where he was and was not interested in getting new directions. He insisted someone needed to come and get him. I quickly volunteered, not wanting to take my fiancé away from the rest of his family. They lived so far away and he rarely saw them. Plus, he hadn't been in town long enough to have a clue where he was either.

I knew exactly where they were calling from and could be there and back in just a few minutes. No one argued and I headed back out the door. I was at the intersection they had specified within five minutes, but there was no one around. I spent the next thirty minutes scouring the neighborhood for any sign of the car they were driving. I eventually returned to the restaurant just as the meal ended and was of course relieved my brother-in-law and his family had made it without my guidance. As the night ended my husband's best man assured me again that they would be at the chapel on time. We said goodnight and spent our last night single with our families.

The morning of our wedding was beautiful. Everyone was up early. It was the perfect fall day. The leaves were the most beautiful I have ever seen during fall in Tennessee. My mother and my sister left early, leaving my father to drive me to the chapel. It was nice having that last moment with my dad on my wedding day.

The pre-wedding activity was ordered chaos. I hid out in the bride's room. When the photographer arrived the real frenzy began. I took pictures with everyone including the groundskeeper! My favorite, except for the ones taken with my groom, was the one of me in my ivory wedding gown on an antique sofa with my precious little nephew sitting beside me. He had the sweetest little smile.

Nine years old and absolutely adorable in his tuxedo, he was doing just fine. Jesse had been right. Somehow things just work out. Not always the picture we would have drawn, but when you pull back and see all the detail, the tapestry God weaves is so much more beautiful than the little doodles we try to make of our lives.

They strategically transported me back to the bride's room as soon as the photographer was finished. With relief I knew my groom had finally arrived. As we had left the room to walk around the grounds, they seemed unconcerned that my fiancé and I would accidentally cross paths. Honestly, that had concerned me. It was getting late and I was still a little concerned that he might decide to leave me at the altar, even though his brothers had insisted that they would not allow that to happen. He would show up or they would kill him. They made it clear. They would not be dragged all the way to Tennessee without a wedding taking place. I was starting to understand the description "Yooper" more and more. What it really meant was Northern Redneck!

The moments before our wedding were some of the longest of my life. My time was spent hiding out, waiting for the cue to exit the building and take my place on the steps outside the main chapel doors. This place was and still is so beautiful. It was like something out of a picture book of fairytales; and on my wedding day, I felt like the fairytale could come true. As the doors opened and my father escorted me down the aisle, the day was everything I could have hoped for. I had somehow completely forgotten the whispered conversations I had overheard just moments earlier about missing shoes, ugly dresses, and the cake. For a fleeting moment, I remembered the mess my cat had made of our wedding cake and wondered what the outcome had been. As I saw my groom waiting for me at the altar, the wedding cake slipped from my mind again. It could have been made of Twinkies and I couldn't have cared less.

With the exception of the ornate chapel our wedding was much like all Southern country weddings. My uncle performed the ceremony. This was the same uncle that had harbored my sister and my nephew in Maine almost ten years earlier. They had recently moved south to Georgia. He traveled the country starting churches in areas where churches were few and far between. He was a preacher and my father's brother, which meant he was never short on words. I think we must have forgotten that small detail when we told him there would be a lot of Catholics in attendance, and we wanted to make them feel comfortable. We mentioned they were accustomed to a more formal and longer ceremony than was typical of a Southern wedding.

This was another one of those, "What were you thinking?" moments. I don't know what I was thinking when I encouraged my uncle to stretch out the ceremony a little. "Don't rush it," I said. So, almost an hour after I joined my future husband at the altar, he was still my future husband. There was one point in the ceremony when I was concerned we would be there longer than our rental agreement allowed.

I realized just how long we had been standing there when I was instructed to hand a rose to my future mother-in-law just before taking our vows. I had presented a rose to my mother as my father brought me down the aisle; and now I was to give one to my husband's mother. My uncle had spoken so long that the stem of her rose had broken as I struggled to hang on to the single rose along with my bouquet. Fortunately, she and I both giggled as I passed her the rose; and the pitiful little bloom fell over as she took it from my hand.

Finally, the exchanging of vows and the pronouncement that we were husband and wife sent cheers throughout the chapel. I am not sure if it was for our marriage or the simple fact that the guest knew the ceremony had finally ended. As Southern tradition dictates, the crowd was directed to the reception room for a quiet reception of punch, peanuts, mints, and cake. The cake! I had almost forgotten about the cake.

chapter 26

Two Receptions, the Cat and a Honeymoon

By the time my husband and I had entered the reception area, the festivities were in full swing. Punch was being served in delicate glass cups by my pretty little newly-acquired nieces. One had served double duty as my flower girl as well. Everyone was there, including cousins I had not seen in many years. Even an old friend I had played basketball with had driven in from Kentucky. I was amazed at how many of my new Northern relatives had made the trip and were sticking around for the punch and peanut reception. I thought they would already be on their way to what one of my brothers-in-law had referred to all week as the real reception.

A lot of my co-workers were there. We were like family and I knew something was up when I noticed them going to great lengths to avoid the cake. As it turns out, the co-worker I had ranted to in the hallway two days earlier had decided to go to brunch just before the wedding. He told me later that he didn't mean to say anything, but it is amazing how a champagne brunch can loosen your tongue. Rumor has it, he moved from group to group saying, "Don't eat the cake." And followed it up with, "Meow."

The reception at the chapel wrapped up quickly. The day had been beautiful, but dark clouds were rolling in. As we left the chapel with the car covered in wedding steamers and graffiti, the storm hit. The car was such a mess my new husband stopped at the car wash before we headed to the club for the Yankee reception.

As expected, my new Northern family and a few local friends attended the party. I have to admit, one of the highlights for me was dancing the polka with my brother-in-law, especially since we were dancing across the same floor I had first spotted my new husband on just a little over a year earlier. My husband was an embarrassment to his Polish heritage. He had no idea how to do the polka. He had spent all his free time on the football fields and basketball courts instead of the dance clubs. So, his brother stepped in to initiate me into my new Polish family.

Thankfully no one expected us to stay too long. After an hour, they saw us off and on our way to the Opryland Hotel. Much like our honeymoon destination, the hotel was the most popular wedding nightspot in Tennessee. We pulled into valet parking and checked in. We were still dressed for the wedding, so they gave us VIP treatment. The bellman escorted us to our room and even used our camera to snap a picture of my new hubbie carrying me across the threshold. Within moments, we were standing on our balcony overlooking the incredible waterfalls and conservatory inside the hotel.

As we stood on the balcony, we forgot that since we were dressed in full wedding regalia, looking as though we just stepped off the top of a wedding cake, we might catch the attention of those walking through the hotel gardens. Lost in the moment, we were standing close, whispering, sharing a quiet exhausted kiss until we were interrupted by applause from the crowd gathered below us. We laughed, kissed again, a little showier this time, took a bow, and went inside. Then we ordered pizza. I swear. We were starving. Even with two wedding receptions, we never got a chance to eat. That was the best pizza ever; we still talk about it to this day.

Our honeymoon in the Smoky Mountains was just as you would expect. It was quiet, wonderful, and much too short. We spent the week doing what all tourists do. We took the traditional sky chair lift across the mountaintops and visited Dolly Parton's

Dixie Stampede for dinner. Of course, we had the obligatory Western saloon picture made. The staff at the photo shop selected our costumes. They assured me that I was dressed as a saloon girl and my new husband was a cowboy, but honestly I thought I looked more like a hooker and my husband an outlaw!

Our honeymoon was the same week as the presidential election. We had failed to fill out our absentee ballots, so neither of us voted, something we both usually did without fail. The wedding and the election sneaked up on us and we simply forgot. Having failed to cast our vote, (which we both considered our duty as citizens of this great country) we felt obligated, even on our honeymoon, to at least check out the election returns.

We got distracted pretty quickly. It's not what you think. As we sat watching the returns, we were tinkering with our camera and came to the disappointing realization that all of our great honeymoon pictures would have to live only in our memories. My dad had loaned us a really nice 35mm camera. It was silly for us to assume it was loaded with film. It was not.

So besides the picture taken at the Dixie Stampede and the one where I am dressed as a hooker, our honeymoon pictures are nonexistent. I keep hoping one will show up one day. The gardens were really crowded the night we were caught kissing on our balcony. Everyone carries cameras when they tour the hotel so, I am sure that at least one or two snapped a picture. One of these days, maybe one will show up in the hotel's wedding albums.

It seemed we had only just arrived when it was time to head home. I think the drive home was one of the strangest moments of my life. It was finally hitting me. I was married! He had gone through with it. He said he loved me; and I loved him. We were both really quiet as we drove across the mountains for one last look. I couldn't help wondering what was going through his mind. It was making me sick just thinking about it. This time last year he was still in love with another woman and now he was married to me.

chapter 26

The silence was killing me. Was he thinking what I was thinking? We got married too quickly? Not that I was thinking that, but I was thinking he was thinking it. I continued to tell myself to just stop it and think about the beautiful mountains, the wonderful week, and the beautiful wedding; but I couldn't help it. That was the battle going on in my head when I should have been relaxed in newlywed bliss.

The uncertainty Jesse and I had talked about just days before the wedding was back with a vengeance. It had been shoved aside during the final days of the wedding and the honeymoon. It is easy to do with the right distraction, but as we headed back to the real world, my real clouds continued to gather. Why couldn't I just be happy? Why did I have to be suspicious about everything? I didn't feel as though I could trust anyone or anything and it was time to figure out why.

chapter 27

Rediscovering "The Church"

As we settled into our new home, we immediately became as busy as ever. My schedule was still crazy and I liked it that way. My husband traveled and when he was away, my insecurities intensified. I trusted him, but I wondered. I knew he loved me, but I also knew women were going to approach a guy like him on the road, wedding ring or not.

I had so much I closed off and kept inside. It seemed the only one I ever opened up to was Jesse. My husband was getting to know Jesse too and he encouraged me to keep our relationship alive. He knew I had a lot I kept to myself and he didn't push, at least not yet. I think he saw early on that staying friends with Jesse was going to be important. He knew I needed someone to talk to and, until I was ready to really open up to him, listening seemed to be Jesse's specialty.

Our lives changed so much, and in such a short amount of time. I was prepared for our first year together to have some rough spots, but it was mostly bliss. My husband was still traveling, working for the company out of Michigan. He had given up on law enforcement. The academy had called, but the timing was wrong. They called him and asked him to report just two weeks before our wedding. He saw that as a sign that he was on the wrong path. He was already considering a different road and that had sealed the deal in his mind; but I am not so sure it had in mine.

Working as he had for a roofing manufacturing company, he decided he had gained enough technical experience to go into business for himself. No one knew the specifications and installation guidelines as he did and he was very good. I knew he could do the work, but I was not convinced I wanted to own a small business. I had grown up in the farming industry. I saw first-hand how difficult life could be for an entrepreneur, but his heart was set on it.

With his plans now moving toward business ownership, we immediately began looking for a house with a little room to grow. We found it north of Nashville and moved just six months after our wedding. We were still in full honeymoon mode, but were starting to take strides toward our extended professional future. I continued to work as much as possible in an industry I loved. I talked of finishing my degree, but after the wedding, then the move, and now starting a business, I decided my degree could wait; and it did for over twenty years.

Another big change within our first year of marriage was a desire to reconnect with a faith-based community. You would call it "church." I have never been fond of the word "church." The "church" had let me down in so many ways, so many times. It was much later before I began to fully understand the magnitude of my discontent.

We began visiting churches. That was a miserable time. We felt awkward and obvious and guarded. It's no wonder so many just sleep in on Sunday morning. Half the churches we visited were in the middle of fund-raising campaigns. There is nothing more disconcerting for a prospective new member than a church begging for money on your first visit.

Other congregations seemed almost robotic, just going through the motions. Some were just downright depressing, as though God wants us to live a life of misery to keep us longing for the joy of heaven. None of it seemed right.

One church we had not yet visited was high on my list. It was famous in the tribe I had worshiped with my entire life. I had heard so much about their famous song leaders and the connections they had to the music industry, but more than that I was in awe of their size. At one time they were the biggest in the country and I simply wanted to see it for myself. I never thought this would be the place we would hang our hat; it was simply too large. My husband and I had grown up under different Christian banners, but we were both from small congregations where everyone knew each other.

The morning we visited the super church everything was just as it should be to draw us in. The people were friendly, not pushy. We saw evidence of extensive community outreach and programs for everyone in need. They had a preacher that seemed to speak right to our hearts. He made more sense to me in that first visit than anyone had in a very long time and he seemed sincere. Insincerity is something I never seemed to notice early in life, but now I could spot it a mile away.

We felt at home from that very first day and signed up for classes to help us understand everything they had to offer. We soon found that what they had to offer was what they allowed us to offer to the world. They had great programs for kids, which we hoped were in our future. They offered some great studies and worship time. But what impressed us most of all was how they were more about what was going on outside the walls than inside. We were home.

chapter 28

Two for One!

We settled into a family rhythm quickly. We both worked Monday through Friday. We worked on home projects and maybe had a date night on the weekend, but Sunday morning we went to worship. One of the benefits to being as tall as my husband and I both are is that people don't forget you. That was the case at worship and within a few weeks of regular attendance we felt as though we had been there for years.

My husband was still working to start a business and would spend some weekends working to make extra cash to buy a truck and the tools he would need to really get things going. We were running our little start-up roofing company out of a small shed he had built in the backyard. We knew once the business really got going, our neighbors and the city codes would insist we move the work out of our residential neighborhood.

About the same time the business was really starting to need more room, so did we. I was expecting our first child, actually our first children. I discovered I was pregnant with twins just as my husband decided it was time to make the leap. He had decided to give his boss a two-week notice and began looking for property to house our business.

The day we deposited his last paycheck was a rough one for me. I was only a couple of months along in my pregnancy and I guess the emotions got the best of me. I had moments when I would cry uncontrollably, absolutely certain the business was a mistake. But I didn't want to destroy my husband's dream. I finally took my concerns to Jesse.

Surprisingly, my husband had talked to Jesse too. Sometimes I forgot they had become lasting friends in the months leading up to our wedding and had stayed in contact since. They had already discussed my anxiety and the concern I had tried so hard to hide.

Jesse was not for or against the business moving forward. He was for us. He said we had to be honest and upfront with each other. I don't think he minded being put in the middle, but the final word of advice to both of us was always, "Do what you do together, really together."

So together, as my due date neared, we made the decision that my work situation must change. The business was beginning to need someone in the office during the day and that was a job suited to a new mom with two babies to care for. The office was in our home and I could juggle the paperwork and phones between the needs of the twins.

The day I went to tell my program director that I would be leaving, I was not sad or concerned, just resolved that I was doing the right thing. It was the right thing for my babies, the right thing for my husband, and the right thing for our business. I don't think I ever thought it was the right thing for me; but motherhood has a way of pushing personal ambitions out of the picture for a time.

I seriously felt no regrets when I met with my boss to reveal my future plans. My primary job was still as a traffic reporter so I worked a split shift. I told him there was no way I could leave two babies at, what we in the broadcast industry refer to as "dark-thirty" in the morning and then again in the middle of the afternoon.

He immediately suggested something I had never thought of - doing my job from home. I knew others who worked from home. I was planning on working from home to help my husband run his business. The idea I could broadcast from home? I could not imagine how they could make that happen, but they did.

Just before the twins were born I was set up with everything I would need to provide traffic updates to my stations from my kitchen table. This was long before the Internet and WiFi connections. The station set up a special phone line, often used in remote broadcasts. It allowed me to have the best of both worlds. I could be with my twins and continue to work in an industry I loved. The continued paychecks provided financial stability as the birth of our twins drew near.

We found ourselves spending more and more time with our spiritual family. We had so much to be thankful for and we wanted God to know we appreciated it. We began attending the Wednesday night Bible study along with our normal Sunday morning worship.

We were building real friendships with some of the other families at the church. They even threw us a baby shower. We spent more and more time listening to the preacher we had admired from the first moment we heard him speak. Then just a few weeks before the twins were born, we were both re-baptized. I had been baptized as a teenager, and I sometimes thought I did it more out of fear than conviction. My husband's entire family was Catholic so he was baptized as an infant in the Catholic Church. As we reflected on our growing spiritual lives, we decided we wanted our baptisms to be something we fully understood. Our lives were about to change forever as we added to our family, and it seemed like a good time for our spiritual lives to make a change as well.

chapter 29

Motherhood? Let the Guilt Begin!

The day the twins were born was an event. I was the traffic reporter on several radio stations in the Nashville area and my pregnancy was part of the show. Speculation was made on when the event would happen, how big the babies would be, and if they would both in fact be boys. We had been told in ultrasounds that they were both indeed male, but as friends and close associates knew, sometimes those forecasts were wrong.

Nonetheless, names were selected (girls names too, just in case), but the nursery was decorated in blue. At my eight-month physical the doctor declared it was time, and instead of waiting till the due date, I was scheduled to induce labor and have our twins two days later. Final plans were made quickly and the twins' birthday arrived.

The local hospital rolled out the red carpet. It seemed as though everyone in town knew this was the day. On-air updates were given and one of our talk show hosts actually called and put me on the air just thirty minutes before our first son was born. The second followed just thirty minutes later and yes, they were both boys.

I can't begin to describe the love I felt for those little ones the moment I laid eyes on them, the love and the fear. You see, I had made great strides in my faith and security, but I was a long way from what I would need to be. I began to worry the moment I discovered I was pregnant. I didn't know how I was going to be able to sleep at night now that I was in charge of two helpless little lives. Also, I knew nothing about babies!

I had grown up the second girl on a farm. So while my sister played house and learned to do what most girls learned to do, I chased after my father outside. Oh, I knew how to deliver and care for newborn pigs, but real live human babies? I had never even baby-sat, not once, and the dolls my mother had given me as a child were in mint condition. My old dolls are probably worth a fortune, because they look as though they were never touched. When most little girls were playing with dolls and dreaming of the mothers they would be, I was digging worms to sell at a road-side bait stand. I swear it's the absolute truth!

I was worried during my pregnancy. I didn't think I could do it. I didn't have a clue. The day the hospital was getting us ready to go home, I asked my mom, "Are they really going to let me leave here with two babies? Don't they know I don't know what I'm doing?" My mother laughed. Mom actually laughed at me a lot those first months. I guess she knew I would figure it out; and she reassured me the hospital was not concerned that I might not be up to the challenge.

She was right. They let me leave, and they never seemed the least bit concerned. There wasn't a test or license I had to have. Honestly, as I sat there getting ready to leave I thought, How can they make such a big deal about learning to drive a car and care less about whether or not someone so inexperienced should be entrusted with another human life? No, let me correct that - two human lives! I guess they knew, just as my mom knew, that I would simply do what came naturally. Somehow, God gave me the skills I needed for the job.

The first weeks home were a little chaotic. Having arrived a month early the twins had some minor health issues that didn't allow us to simply enjoy new parenthood. I had only arranged to take two weeks off after the birth. By the time we had the boys set-tled into their new home, it was time for me to get back to work.

Since I worked from home, I could see no reason to stay out any longer. With only one secure income, we needed the money.

The constant activity gave us no time to think or rethink anything we did. By the time the twins were a month old, we were pros. I took the babies everywhere. They accompanied me to remote broadcasts and special events around town. I became gifted at pushing one shopping cart with baby carriers inside while pulling another cart with groceries.

Every milestone was an event. One twin walked several months before the other. The one that took his time learning to walk went from crawling straight to running. I loved taking the twins to their dad's job sites when he was working in town. He was still traveling because many of the jobs he secured were too far from home to justify coming home every night.

On my nights alone with the twins, I stayed on the phone with my husband until he was so tired that I could hear sleep in his voice. Even with twins to care for, sleep was still something I had a hard time with. Unless I was exhausted, I couldn't shut down my mind. So, many of the nights I couldn't sleep were spent just like my childhood, talking to Jesse. I was blissfully happy, but still had something locked inside of me that would not allow me to completely trust anyone. My insecurities ran deep through a lifetime of uncertainty and distrust.

Even with a husband that was a devoted father to our boys and obviously passed out exhausted when he was out of town, I had a hard time trusting him when he was away. It was during one of those long nights alone after a long talk with Jesse that I began to understand at least a part of it. Hadn't I been a part of another woman's betrayal? Shouldn't that action make me unworthy of a faithful husband? Maybe it wasn't so much my distrust that was the problem; maybe it was my guilt and what I considered a justified harvest for what I had sown.

I did not share my revelation with my husband. He knew about everything I had done. We had no secrets. I think being friends for as long as we were helped us to open up to each other without the fear of rejection, but I was not ready to tell him I felt that I deserved an unfaithful husband. I did however share this information with Jesse and he, of course insisted that I was off my rocker! Never did he think for a minute that I deserved anything but a faithful, loving husband no matter what I had done or thought I did. Still it ate at me. I would lay awake for hours imagining how God would deliver His just retribution.

chapter 30

Country to the Core – The Big Move

As the twins celebrated their first birthday, we were finally ready to move our growing family and business to more suitable accommodations. An abandoned farm just thirty minutes north-west of Nashville proved just the place. It is still the most beautiful piece of property in our county, in my opinion.

The location is convenient to everything. The place should be worth a small fortune. The only reason we were able to afford it was due to the wastewater plant across the field. It reduced the property value low enough that it was in our price range. Our friends love the farm, but love to tease us too. Not many people choose to move next door to a sewer plant. I remind them that I grew up on a hog farm and would rather live next to the plant than a livestock barn. So for me, it was an easy sale and, for the record, they have been great neighbors.

There were several old buildings on the property but none that were inhabitable. The farm is believed to be one of the original area homesteads started in the late 1700's. There was an old cabin on the property that had been built around that same time period, but only the chimney remains. Another was a shack that had at one time housed a family, but now served as a storage shed for things you wanted out of sight, but were too lazy to take to the dump. The old barns were in great shape, but were not exactly the type of buildings you could move into and set up house, especially with two one-year-old little boys.

We needed a house built quickly and decided to have one moved to the property. Not one of those prefab houses. This was a house that had been condemned due to noise issues near the Nashville Airport. The guy we bought it from removed the brick, picked it up, and moved it from Nashville to our farm. It was an amazing process to watch. Instant house. We had to build the foundation and the lower basement level; but otherwise, they moved it and did the final attachment to the new foundation.

On the day of the actual move, I watched as the house was maneuvered at a slow crawl under traffic lights and around tight corners. It was really fascinating. I had always wondered what crazy person has a house moved and why. Now I know. We bought the house and had it moved for just ten thousand dollars.

The only problem was a neighbor at the end of our road. We needed permission to drive across their yard because of the angle of the turn. I called and obtained the consent we needed, assuring them we would repair any possible damage to the lawn when we were finished. They were really nice and gave us permission without any hesitation, but the morning of the move they had a little different attitude.

The house was being moved in two large sections. We moved the first section through their yard without any problems. The grass looked untouched, not even the slightest tire track was evident. Then just as the second section of the house was making its way across the yard, our neighbors yelled for us to stop.

The man of the house ran out waving his arms saying his yard could not take the stress. He said we could not move the rest of the house across his property. I don't remember exactly what I said, but I do remember the stress I had experienced all day. Now, just a mile and a half from our farm, this guy was suddenly a problem.

I quickly decided that we were far enough out in the country that I could leave the house sitting right where it was. It might even take me a day or two to sort it all out with the local sheriff's office.

I decided I could wait. I think my neighbor realized the predicament as well, when I looked at him and said, "Well, I hope you like where it is, because I can leave it right here. Or if you'd rather, we can keep moving and be out of your way in just a few minutes."

My neighbor with the extra house sitting in his yard decided rather quickly not to call my bluff, and soon we were on our way. The rest of the process moved very quickly. It is really amazing how quickly a house can be attached to the foundation and look as though it was built there in the first place. We still had a lot of renovations to do, but with the time we saved picking up a house and moving it, we were country-dwellers once again before the fall.

I loved our farm from the moment we spent our first night there. My husband worked hard and we quickly had things running efficiently. We added porches on the front and back of the house. One of the old barns was renovated into office space; and the old livestock barn became the warehouse for our roofing company.

Inside the house, we moved walls and doors and custom built a radio studio with a playroom for the kids. I no longer had to do traffic from my kitchen table, but from a studio nicer than the ones we had in Nashville. We even installed soundproof windows overlooking the playroom so I could watch the boys while I worked. It was again the best of both worlds. I loved it and so did the twins.

chapter 31

The Rock Star and Resolutions

About six months after we moved to the farm, we decided it was time to find a local church. We were still attending services in Nashville but doubted we would stay faithful with such a long drive. We started the process of looking for a new congregation. We met some great people, but we had already spent too much time with the congregation in Nashville. Nothing else felt right and we missed our friends. So, after a year-long absence, we made the decision to commute.

When we returned, everything seemed to be just as we had left it. We jumped right back into our classes and soon we were feeling that little something you feel when you know you are on the right track again. Everything felt just right. Not long after our return, the congregation had a special series scheduled with a former atheist, now Christian. He traveled the country sharing his journey with others. He was a physics and science teacher and shared the scientific evidences of God's existence.

I couldn't believe it. This was something I had needed since childhood. I had always believed in God, but it felt more like a "default setting" than a real belief. I believed just in case He was what everyone had taught me He was. My mind could not wrap around a real concept of God; it never had. At least, not in the time I had lived as a person capable of true independent thought. As a child, I believed because my parents said so and that was enough. But growing up in the sixties and seventies, in a time of radical questions with very few real answers, I spent many sleepless nights wide awake in doubt.

My doubts grew with my early interest in archaeology and geology. My dad loved to travel, and one of the best trips we ever took was out West to the Grand Canyon. Seeing the geological record visible throughout the canyon and the obvious age of the planet caused me to question the timelines we had been taught to embrace in Bible school. The earth was much older than many wanted to believe. The dinosaur skeletons were tangible evidence of the earth's age as well. I had so many questions that for so many years had gone unanswered.

I remember the first night of the seminar as though it were yesterday. My husband was on an out-of-town job. He had asked what my plans were for the week and seemed a bit surprised that I planned to drive into Nashville every evening for the program. They were providing free childcare, so he saw no reason for me to miss it. I don't think he fully understood how desperately I had been waiting for this opportunity.

As the lecture began, I was immediately struck with how Northern the speaker sounded. Being married to a "Yankee" gave me an appreciation of their typical bluntness and frank way of speaking. This gentleman was a riot. I loved his ability to get straight to the point. From the very moment he said his first words he pulled me into his message completely. By the time the seminar was over, I felt like a groupie. I found myself hanging around for just a moment to talk with the star of the show and asking question after question about details I didn't quite understand.

The object of my admiration was direct, but kind, with a dry sense of humor. You could tell he was accustomed to dealing with fans like myself and spent as much time as needed to take my questions. He would often answer my question by giving me material to study and directions on where to find the answers I needed. He was every bit the teacher, but to me, he was a rock star.

I can't properly describe the effect his seminar had on me. It was as though a cloud that had been hanging over my entire presence, for my entire life, suddenly lifted. No longer did I believe in God because Mom and Dad, and so many others that I loved and respected, said so. I believed because He was real.

My husband noticed a difference in me immediately. I spent hours sharing with him every detail I had learned. I showed him the material I had been given and, before long, I was seeing the same certainty in his eyes that I now saw in my own.

Jesse was thrilled. He had known about my doubts since childhood. He had tried to help me work through them. He had a faith that I could never understand. It was strong and certain in good times and in bad. It was actually the strongest when he struggled. My husband and I spent many hours studying together, studying with Jesse, and continuing to see our spiritual lives grow.

I had fewer sleepless nights; but with my newfound fire for God and what He wanted for my life, I began to worry again about the wild oats I had sown. That was a life I had left long ago and had no desire to return to it. But the guilt would not let me go. I still had a gut-wrenching fear that I would one day have to harvest what I had planted.

Not long after my new birth of conviction, our preacher presented a lesson that struck right at the core of my restlessness. As he delivered the sermon, he spoke of the tragedy of a life spent in guilt over something God had long since forgiven. As he said it, I thought he was speaking directly to me. I got a knot in my stomach that would not go away as he continued the lesson. He said the key to getting beyond the guilt we insist on carrying is letting God know we need Him to help us get past it. He advised praying for exactly what we needed. He encouraged us not to be vague, but bold in our prayers, and to cry out to God to help us work through anything that might haunt us and hold us prisoner, keeping us from the life God wants for us.

chapter 31

After the sermon I told my husband how the message affected me. He knew I had problems with trust and part of it was because of the guilt I felt and the punishment I believed I deserved. We had fought on more than one occasion, when I would question him over and over about his activities on the road. I was certain he must have strayed, not because I thought he was that type of husband, but because I deserved it.

We talked and he agreed to pray with me for peace and a way to finally forgive myself and move on. Jesse was on board as well. He agreed. Pray for exactly what I needed. He said God already knows, but sometimes our path to healing is only blocked by our unwillingness to ask God for help. He said sometimes we think we don't deserve the healing, so we don't ask. That night I prayed, "God I know you forgave me long ago, now please show me how to forgive myself." I felt better that night. I still felt guilty, but I felt that I was finally on the right track to making peace with myself.

chapter 32

A Harvest of Forgiveness

Over the course of about two weeks, I prayed the same prayer several times a day. I finally understood what Scripture meant when it said, "pray without ceasing." With my new confidence that God was there and He was listening, I talked to Him all the time. Every conversation included my plea for peace and relief from the guilt I had carried for so many years.

During this same time period, we were experiencing some mechanical trouble with a satellite dish. This was one of the old ones about the size of a truck. We had purchased it shortly after our move to the country. A technician had worked on it for several days and finally, in frustration, asked if he could bring his brother out to consult on the problem. I agreed and thought no more about it until the next day when I answered a knock at my door.

I opened the door and nearly fainted. There on my steps, smiling like an old friend was the object of my guilt. The married man I had briefly dated was standing right in front of me. I had not seen or heard from him since I ended the relationship all those years ago and now here he was.

After opening the door and realizing immediately who was standing in front of me, I froze. I don't even remember saying hello. If he recognized me, he didn't mention it. He didn't introduce himself, but simply explained he was there to help his brother and would let me know as soon as they determined the problem. He continued to explain, if the issues were minor, they would go ahead and make the repair without consulting with me further.

I may have said "thank you," "OKAY," or something else, but I don't remember doing so. I quickly shut the door and went to the corner of my kitchen and started praying. Why did I go to the corner of my kitchen? I have no idea, but it seemed to be the spot where I could block out everything else and just shout out, "God, what is this? This obviously has something to do with my prayer, but what do you want me to do?"

I couldn't imagine and He was not talking, at least not in the way He did back in the days of Moses. I was really hoping for a "burning bush" moment or some moment of clarity. It was certainly part of what I had been praying about, but it was way out of my realm of understanding.

The twins were sound asleep taking their naps. I had checked on them just before the knock at the door, so I stood in the corner and prayed until I heard another knock. I took a deep breath and looked up. I guess I was hoping God would wink, wave, something, anything to help me out, but it was still just me. Me talking to God, asking for guidance, and getting completely freaked out by who I knew was standing on my steps, waiting for me to answer the door.

Finally, I went to the door and invited the brothers inside. I said nothing (nothing to my guest), but God and I were having a long talk in my head. We all sat down and the man from my past immediately grinned and began to say how good it was to see me again. He had obviously recognized me as well. He continued by telling his brother how we had once dated and then turned to me and said, "Yeah, I'm married now and have a son." As those words came out of his mouth, "liar" rang in my head.

At that moment his brother got a phone call from his office. We sat and listened to a one-sided conversation that went something like this. "Yeah, he's here. No, he doesn't want to talk to you." The brothers passed a knowing look between them, as if they both knew what the phone call was about. "Okay, fine just a minute," he continued, handing the phone to his brother. "Just talk to her for a minute," he said, insisting his brother take the call. With a shrug he begrudgingly took the phone.

Now, the one-sided conversation was clear, on the other end of the phone was another, other woman. It hit me with such clarity that I could feel the rage building up inside of me. He was still a creep.

As he ended the call, he began reminiscing again, attempting to return to the lies and stories he was telling a moment earlier. I interrupted him and said, "I remember you too and you have haunted my dreams." Misunderstanding my meaning, he smiled smugly until I continued. "No, make that my nightmares," I added quickly. His expression changed immediately.

I said, "I know that you are married just as you were back then, and I am so sorry for my part in that relationship. It was wrong and it tears me up inside. I can't stop thinking about your wife and what a horrible thing I was a part of." It was his turn to be speechless. So I continued. "As a matter of fact I would love to have the opportunity to apologize to her, if you would allow me." Still not knowing how to respond, he simply sat there for a moment, stunned. Finally, his brother intervened. He handed me the bill, explained briefly what was done, accepted my check, and they both practically ran out my door. I have never seen nor heard from either of them again.

As the door shut behind them, so did the door to my guilt. In its place was a doorway to forgiveness. Not forgiveness from God (I had that long ago), but forgiveness from myself. Maybe now I could open the door and find the pathway to forgiving others.

I had a hard time going to sleep I was so excited. I had to replay every detail for my husband and, yes, Jesse too. We were in awe of how quickly and how clearly God had answered my prayer. I am still ashamed of what I did, but no longer does guilt haunt my spirit. It was another new beginning for me. A new beginning of real and certain trust, not just with my husband, but also trust that I would one day be able to deal with the hate and resentment I had buried so deep for so long.

chapter 32   141

jesse

chapter 33

The Pathway Home

Every milestone emboldened me. I was certain that, just as God had given me a way to overcome my guilt, He would also make a way for me to go home. Not to the home I had made with my husband and children or with my spiritual family in Nashville, but home to Kentucky where I left a piece of my heart so long ago.

That is not to say we didn't visit. Of course we did, my entire family is there. But there was always a resentment clouding my time in Kentucky and a certainty that I would never feel at home there again. The wounds were too deep.

As I continued to see my faith and spiritual life build, so did my understanding of the events from the past. Jesse and I talked more and more about the details I had shared only with him. As I began to revisit old wounds he revisited old advice—advice he had given me from the beginning. Hurt leads to hate and hate, left to its own devices, will eat away at your heart and soul.

Jesse always said that the only way to deal with hurt and hate is head on and the first step in my head-on collision with my past was to make sure my husband knew it all. We didn't have secrets, but I did have emotional scars that I hesitated to share. Jesse had always encouraged me to open up to my husband, especially as their relationship grew. They had become good friends; and he constantly reassured me that I could trust him. Still, I wasn't ready.

Dealing with tough issues is not something you just dump at someone's feet, especially during a time of joy. That was where we were as a family, in a time of great joy. So I wasn't exactly stalling when Jesse urged me to share the details and depth of my hurt with my husband. I just didn't want to think on those things as our family of four was expanding to five. Our third son was born just four days before Christmas. The twins were three and a half years old.

We barely had time to get used to a five-member household when our fourth son was born in the winter, fourteen months after the third. It was amazing how two more little souls could add so much to an already bursting household, but they certainly did. Now with four boys, ages four and a half and younger, our family was complete and we settled into a joyous and wonderful time.

I look back now at the videos and pictures of my boys' child-hoods. We had fun. We did it right. We played, we sang, we danced, and drank in every moment we could. I have no regrets, but that is not to say that we did not make some colossal mistakes. We made some that stun me to this day. Rather than making excuses for the mistakes, we learned quickly that, if we would allow Him, God would grow us and grow our children through those tough times.

Over the course of the past thirty years, God has shown me over and over that all things can work for good to those who love God. That doesn't mean that all things are good, just that He can work with it, if you will let Him. That was what He did for me. Once I was finally ready to allow it, He turned it all around and showed me the pathway home.

My boys were still very young when I finally began to make real progress. It was rough at first. One of my biggest break-throughs came in the middle of a movie one night. We were watching a show centered on racial conflict. If I had realized what the movie was about, I probably would have avoided it altogether. Our boys had never dealt with anything racial. They were close to their cousin and thought no more of his dark skin than they did of my frequently-changing hair color. It was just a color.

The twins had asked a few questions. When they started school, things were said that promoted an awareness of a difference between races in some families; but it was still something they simply could not understand. They had never experienced anything but their family, and their family was not one color.

As we sat and watched the movie, I began several times to tear up and I knew my family was noticing. The movie came to an abrupt ending for us when a scene was shown with graffiti painted across a fence outside the home of one of the characters in the movie. The words were, of course, hurtful and racist. The scene was no worse than several that had already occurred, but something about that scene set me off.

Seeing how upset I had become, my husband shut off the movie and we began to talk. I talked to my family in a way that night that I was never sure I could. I shared with them my hurt, my anger, and my hatred. Hatred that I had held in so long that it had become a part of me. Really talking about it with those closest to me was a big step in letting it go.

I had started to heal several years earlier as I learned to move past my own guilt and forgive myself. Jesse and I had talked at length about my need to forgive what had happened back in Kentucky if I ever hoped to put it behind me. I began to make the effort. Parts of the process were easier than others. So many I loved and trusted were simply at fault for doing nothing. Time had allowed me to see clearly how difficult doing the right thing can be when staying silent or uninvolved is an option.

This was one of the key events God used to His glory in my life. That experience made me an activist. I have never been one to stay silent when problems arise and I teach my children to speak up and help out as well. Never in a violent way, but in a way that shows God to the world.

Some of the people from back home were not as easy to forgive. They were hard and hateful and mean. It was also a time that taught me to forgive and then to pity them. Not with a spiteful kind of pity, but with a heart of grief and pity for a spirit so broken and misguided. Another life lesson I taught my children was that those who try to hurt us will always be in our lives. Don't fear them; pity them, then pray for them.

I began to share more and more with my family and as I did the layers of hate began to peel away. Just as the guilt I had carried for so many years had lifted once I learned to forgive myself, the hatred left when I learned to forgive others.

That night my husband and I talked with Jesse. We told him what had happened. I could hear his smile as he congratulated me on beginning to break free. We had been down such a long, dark road together and I was finally seeing the light once again. Jesse said what I was thinking. I had been in the clouds far too long and now the light was almost blinding.

chapter 34

A Testimony

As I began to live life without the weight of bitterness and hate, my mind became more creative and open. I began to write, something that had never occurred to me to do. My boys were growing up way too fast, and I wanted to preserve their childhood. I decided to write about their lives. The idea quickly became children's stories and opened a whole new world for me. I began to write more and more.

If you had told me in high school that I would one day want to be a writer, I would have laughed in your face. I didn't even write my speeches. At least not word for word. Speaking was something that came as easily as breathing for me. I hated tediously writing out every word that I was going to say because I never stuck to the script anyway. It had never occurred to me that if I could find the words for a speech, then I might be able to find the words to write as an author would.

After the children's stories, I wrote a couple of short stories and soon found myself working on some spiritual projects. As my interest in writing grew, so did my interest in Christian and creation evidences. I had studied several books and programs on the subject and found most of the work still missing a few of my key questions. No one seemed to tackle the question, "Why did God create us to fall in the first place?" Couldn't He have just made us perfect and saved us all a lot of grief?

I wanted to know, "Why do we study the Bible? What really makes it so special?" And the list went on and on. I began to look for additional material to study. One opportunity was presented at my congregation. It was a study called *Believing God* by Beth Moore. Believing that He says what He means and means what He says.

I loved the class from the very start. Several of us would stay after the class ended, discussing the material. One night the study was focusing on a topic that I was very familiar with, "Learning to Forgive Yourself." As the class ended, I noticed a friend sitting very quietly. She appeared to be lost in her thoughts. We began to talk, and I found out we shared a similar problem. She was also finding it tough to forgive herself for something that had happened in her life. I immediately shared my story with her. I told her I had felt just like she was feeling and that I knew from experience that God would help her sort it all out. But she had to ask Him for help.

I told her about the man from my past showing up completely unexpectedly only two weeks after I began to pray specifically for guidance. I cautioned her that it might take her longer to work through what she was dealing with or that the answer could come quickly. It was up to her to start the process and ask. I told her that this was what God meant when He said, "knock and the door will opened," but He was clear that it is up to us to knock.

She thanked me for the story and for the encouragement, but still seemed as if she were not buying any of it. I told her I would pray for her as well and that we would talk later. I never asked her what she did nor did I ask for any details about what was bothering her. It never occurred to me to ask. It simply didn't matter.

That week I prayed several times for God to show her how to find peace and finally forgive herself, just as I had. My parents came into town over the next weekend and as usual, they wanted to make a quick stop by the local Christian bookstore. A friend of mine owns the store, and they always have an extensive selection of consignment books in their basement. My mom is an avid reader and loves spending time picking through the shelves.

We had been in the store for about thirty minutes. My short attention span sent me wandering through the rest of the store as I waited on my parents. I began looking through a section of books by one of my favorite authors. I thought I had read everything he had written, but as I searched through his titles, I found one I had never seen. It was *Tilly*, by Frank Peretti. I took it to the counter and asked my friend if it was new. He told me it had been out for several years and, if I enjoyed the author's work, I should read it. I had several books I needed to finish before buying another, but I couldn't resist.

I bought the book, but promised myself I was not going to read it until I finished the ones I had already started. I had a stack of books next to my bed. I set the new edition aside and started reading a book that I had started a couple of days earlier. I read the same page three times and finally gave in. My new purchase was a really short book, and I loved the author, so I decided to skim the pages quickly. I wanted to get a feel for the story.

It only took me about ten minutes to realize it was about a woman coming to terms with an abortion she had when she was younger. As I read through it, I understood so clearly why the author had written the story. I had several friends who had dealt with this issue and I knew I would recommend the book to them. As I continued to flip through the book, I was reminded of my years on Christian university campuses and how I knew abortion was a huge problem. Students would have an abortion rather than face the disciplinary actions from the school, their parents, or the wrath of the church.

As I continued to flip through the pages, I got the funniest feeling. I can't explain it. It was an overwhelming understanding that I had not bought this book for myself. I had bought it for my friend. We had never discussed what she was having a hard time forgiving herself for, but in that moment, I knew. I had never been so certain of anything in my life.

I considered getting into the car and driving over to her house and just handing it to her. The weather was a little icy, and I decided that would be a bad idea at eleven-thirty at night. We had our class the next morning before worship service and it could wait until then. I don't think I slept more than a few hours that night. I was so overwhelmed by how quickly God was reaching out to her. He made me wait a couple of weeks.

The next morning I got to Bible study early. I watched for my friend and as soon as she came into the classroom, I pulled her aside into a spare room. I didn't know how to begin, so I just blurted it out. "Did you have an abortion?" She looked at me absolutely stunned for a moment and then she began to cry. Through tears she said, "How could you possibly know that? My dad is the only one I have ever told." I gave her a hug and said "God told me. This is yours," I added, placing the book in her hands.

Then I told her the whole story. How I had prayed for her that week, my trip to the bookstore with my parents, and the unexpected discovery of the book. I told her it was so odd. I had discovered Frank Peretti several years earlier and had searched through his section many times in my friend's bookstore and other stores as well. How was it possible I had never seen *Tilly* until now?

I told her how overwhelming the feeling of certainty was that I experienced when I realized the book was meant for her, not me. I told her that I was so overwhelmed I that nearly paid her a late night visit the night before. She was almost speechless and just shook her head, staring at the book in her hands. We both fully understood that God had answered her prayer in a very big way; now it was up to her to listen.

chapter 35

Always Remember and Never Forget

I continued attending this same Bible study for several weeks. Every week the instructor encouraged us to memorize Bible verses. She said that when you have key verses committed to memory, it will help you stay focused during tough moments or help you to find peace and encouragement when stresses arise. She said that as we read, we should look for verses that speak directly to us, ones that we can claim as our own.

I had never thought about the importance of memorizing Scripture before. As a kid, it was an exercise we participated in every week in Sunday school. We memorized them without putting an emphasis on what the words meant. The exercise of memorizing Scripture became much like the process of memorizing dates for a history test. Something I would do for the class, then forget.

The class notes recommended a few verses to memorize, but they didn't have any real meaning to me, so I decided to look for my own. We were going through a really tough time in our business, and I seemed to be in a constant turmoil of stress and worry. With the life experiences I had already been through, I was now more aware of what God was teaching me during times of trials. Having an understanding that I was going through a teachable moment never helped me face situations without the worry and stress associated with those times. At least I knew I was learning something and would eventually appreciate the lesson.

Still, in the middle of a struggle it was becoming more and more apparent that one of the biggest issues that God was trying to grow me through was learning to trust Him. I once read a book written by Bodie and Brock Thoene which said that when we refuse to trust God, we are basically calling Him a liar. He tells us over and over that we can trust Him. When we fail to, are we saying He is lying?

Over the years, I know that not trusting God is my most frequent sin. So I thought it appropriate to find a verse to help me with that issue. One morning during an unrelated study, I found exactly what I was looking for was in the letter Paul wrote to the church at Philippi. "Do not be anxious about anything, but in every situation, by prayer and petition, with thanksgiving, present your requests to God. And the peace of God, which transcends all understanding, will guard your hearts and your minds in Christ Jesus" (Philippians 4:6, 7).

Those verses quickly became my mantra; and the instructor was right. They gave me peace. I still worry too much; but those verses remind me that peace is there, if I will simply reach out for it and sincerely claim it.

chapter 36

The Circle Above the Earth

Throughout my life, God has shown Himself to me in big ways, almost always when I least expected it. One of the most beautiful moments in my life came at the same time as my newly found enthusiasm for memory verses and the "God moment" I had shared with my friend over the book *Tilly*.

During the study, we were reading a passage of Scripture that struck me in a way that I can't explain. It was when the prophet Isaiah admonished the children of Israel for their lack of faith in what God can do. This last verse is one of the most familiar passages in Scripture, Isaiah 40:31 "But those who wait upon the LORD will renew their strength. They will soar on wings as eagles; they will run and not grow weary, they will walk and not be faint." I have always loved that verse, but until then, I had never noticed the ten verses that preceded the well-known Isaiah passage.

The twenty-second verse talks about God sitting "enthroned above the circle of the earth." I guess because of the creation evidence studies I had done for several years, it painted a picture in my mind that I could really relate to and understand. I envisioned God sitting above the circle of the earth, keeping a watchful eye over His creation.

Over the course of several days, I began to commit the eleven verses to memory. Late one night, the kids and my husband were already in bed, but as usual, I was not tired. I have always had a tough time getting to sleep. It didn't always mean I was worried about something. I just have a really hard time shutting off my brain to sleep unless I am exhausted. Since I was wide-awake, I decided to work on my memory verses.

I recited the verses I knew over and over, but I continued to stumble on verse 26, "Lift your eyes and look to the heavens: Who created all these? He who brings out the starry host one by one, and calls them each by name. Because of his great power and mighty strength, not one of them is missing." I decided to step outside onto my upstairs deck and see if the night air would help the verse settle into my mind. As I stepped out the door, I started over with verse twenty-two. "He sits enthroned above the circle of the earth, and its people are like grasshoppers. He stretches out the heavens like a canopy, and spreads them out like a tent to live in. He brings princes to naught and reduces the rulers of this world to nothing. No sooner are they planted, no sooner are they sown, no sooner do they take root in the ground, than he blows on them and they wither, and a whirlwind sweeps them away like chaff. 'To whom will you compare me? Or who is my equal?' says the Holy One."

And as I began to test myself on verse twenty-six…"Lift up your eyes look to the heavens, who created all of these…" I naturally looked up at the dark sky.

Immediately overhead, as though I was looking straight into the circle above the earth, was the largest, most defined circle around the moon that I have ever seen.

In the center, the star-filled sky was as clear as crystal and as black as ink. The area outside of the circle was thick with haze. It took my breath away as the verse continued to roll through my mind. "He sits enthroned above the circle of the earth…. Lift your eyes and look to the heavens: Who created all these? He who brings out the starry host one by one, and calls them each by name. Because of his great power and mighty strength, not one of them is missing." I woke everyone up to make sure I wasn't imagining the entire thing. They thought I was crazy. But when they saw the clearly defined circle of the earth, they understood why I was so excited.

Just after they had joined me on the deck, the circle began to fade and within moments it was completely gone. I know that a circle around the moon is a natural phenomenon, but to see one so well-defined at just that moment was incredible.

That night, after everyone had gone back to bed, I was more awake than before. I decided I had to share this with Jesse. As I recanted the entire story, how I had randomly found the verses I was memorizing and the way the circle appeared so clear and perfect for only a few minutes, I was surprised that he stayed silent. I continued talking going back over every detail, and he still had nothing to say. I was shocked. This was such a cool thing. I knew he would think so too, or at least I thought he would, but there was just this awkward silence.

Then unexpectedly, he asked me, "Who am I?" I laughed for a moment until I realized that he was not joking. I said, "You're Jesse." He didn't say anything, so I continued. "You're Jesse, my best friend, my confidant. The best advisor anyone could want." Then he said, "I know what others say. I want to know who I am to you."

Now it was my turn. I didn't know what to say or how to say it. It was another moment of awkward silence until he said again, "Who am I to you?" I could hear the disappointment in his voice, as I remained speechless.

Finally, I said, "You are my best friend, Jesse, for as long as I can remember. I don't remember a time when you weren't there. There is nothing I have ever done that you don't know or understand. You have comforted me and counseled me when no one else would or could."

I stopped talking for a minute then looked up again at the beautiful dark star filled sky. "But you're not Jesse." I finally said, tears filling my eyes, "All these years, it has been easier to hide You behind a childhood friend. You never seemed to mind."

"But you're not a child any longer," He said. "Who am I to you?"

chapter 36   155

"You're my Brother," I confessed. "Not Jesse… You're El Shaddai… My Savior… My Redeemer and my Friend… You're Jesus," I finally said quietly. I could hear the smile in His voice again as He simply said, "I Am"

That night we talked like never before. Childhood friendships are something that I don't think anyone appreciates until they grow old. It is on the look back that you see the way those special friends were woven through every part of your life; and you begin to appreciate them for what they really are. He was there to help me sort out the tough things we all see when our hearts don't understand. He was there to rejoice over the daily miracles and blessings that so often go unnoticed without a friend to share them. He was a friend like that, always there, always loyal, and always taken for granted. Honestly, if we both had not been such social outcasts, I might not have noticed him at all.

epilogue

Some of you may have figured it out long ago or maybe you were just beginning to think that Jesse might actually be Jesus. For years, as I have shared my story, I have often said that when I didn't feel as though I had anyone—I had someone. I prayed all the time, even when my faith faltered. It was only in hindsight that I realized that I never left Jesus because He never left me.

That was the reason I told my story the way I did. He was always there, and the advice He gave me was advice I had learned growing up in a family, community, and a country of faith. Christ taught us everything we needed to know during His short earthly ministry if we will just listen.

Over and over in my story I mention how Jesus—Jesse—advised me. Cleavant Derricks wrote a hymn back in 1937 that beautifully illustrates our interaction throughout my story. "Have a little talk with Jesus… Tell Him all about our troubles… He will hear our faintest cry… and He will answer by and by…" Throughout my life, I have vivid memories of the very different perspectives of my prayer time and the time I spent just talking to Jesus. At the time, I don't think I was consciously aware of the difference; but it was startling. When I began to pray for my sister's unborn child, I prayed to God in a more formal, deliberate manner. It was a prayer I would offer up daily, almost reciting the same verbiage over and over. Then at the conclusion of my prayer I would just talk. Sometimes out loud, if I were alone in my room.

I never wanted anyone to realize how much time I spent alone with my thoughts, seemingly talking to myself, but I always knew someone was listening. Still, I hid my friendship away, afraid others would think I was a Jesus Freak. (A term that is used proudly and fondly now, thanks to the music of DC Talk, but back in the seventies, it meant something completely different.)

I grew up in a time of faith. Almost everyone declared a belief in God. So, it was thought you should keep your God to yourself. No one needed to hear you go on and on about spiritual issues, because we all believed. The thought was, "save it for the mission field," and the United States was not the mission field, or so we thought.

Besides, I was a kid that didn't need to call attention to myself. I already stood out in many ways. I didn't want to add to the list of my idiosyncrasies with terms like "Jesus Freak," "Holy Roller," or "Bible Thumper;" but I carried on an almost constant banter with Jesus. My mind was, and still is, rarely at rest. I was a champion at over-thinking everything and Christ was my sounding board. Just talking it out, whether out loud or clearly in my mind, helped me find peace, even during the toughest moments of my life. When I would feel afraid, discouraged, or confused, I would lay it all out and then sort through it, remembering the Bible lessons I had heard my entire life. I leaned on Christ's teachings without giving it much thought. I had learned the details of His life over and over until they were a part of me. Taking Christ's advice was easy when I was young. As I grew older, I fought more and more against what I knew was right. I often chose in favor of what I wanted rather than what I really needed.

Several of my close friends read *Jesse* before I really ever finished the story. More than one commented on how they felt sorry for Jesse and the way I used his friendship. Of course, it wasn't until the end, when they got the whole picture, that they fully understood. I hid Jesse's identity for that very reason. I wanted to illustrate how Jesus is so often taken for granted. No friend would want to be treated the way I treated Jesse in the story. But honestly, don't we sometimes treat Jesus much worse? We go places we would never take Him. We heap daily praise and worship on the superficial things of this world and then have only a few hours a week for the One who sacrificed everything for us. We don't even introduce Him to our friends.

As the title indicates, this story is true. A couple of times as I recalled details I punctuated them with a statement of absolute truth. I added that because I thought something I had just written sounded so ridiculous it would be thought of as sarcasm.

For the record, I am still married to the "Pretty Man." Our four amazing boys are much older now and my family has healed fully after some tough moments back in the seventies. My nephew is still beautiful, now in his thirties and has an equally beautiful daughter. My sister is no longer married, but happy. They live several hours away and I miss them. I didn't tell much of their story; and it is a story that may still be told, but it is theirs to tell. Not mine.

When I first wrote *Jesse*, the next few sentences read: "The same goes for my parents and my brother. Their story is different than mine, but it is their story. So, while I will say they are happy. I will say no more." Then just five months later Daddy died suddenly of a massive brain hemorrhage.

I thought of not changing the text at all. My family is still happy, just no longer as complete as it once was. Daddy, of course, is completely content and we know that with absolute certainty. Those of us left behind are happy with the cherished memories and the legacy of love with which he blessed us, but our heartbreak is deeply felt. Still, even in heartbreak, we know what's next and the joy of what's to come drives us on.

As far as my family is concerned, we're doing just fine. That is not to say it has all been easy. Remember God uses everything for good if we love Him; but that does not mean everything is good.

My husband eventually closed his business after twenty years. They discovered he had a heart problem several years ago. Nothing that can't be managed, but the process of fully understanding exactly what was wrong with him caused so many hospitalizations and a couple of heart surgeries that he had no choice but to close the company. After a couple of tough years dealing with unemployment, closed doors, and dead ends, he is in the process of changing careers and is going into the insurance industry. It was something neither of us had ever considered until a friend made the suggestion. A suggestion that was made the same week our youth minister presented a lesson urging us to stop telling God what we need and just say, "God, surprise me!" We did and He did and He continues to. I could not be more surprised or proud of what my husband is doing.

The kids? The twins are in college. One is even married! The two youngest are both still in high school. As for me, I still talk to Jesus all the time and He continues to answer just as He did before. In Scripture, in life, and in those crazy moments like the one I experienced at the end of the story looking into the dark sky the night, I realized it was time for my relationship with Christ to change.

That was a powerful moment for me, but it was not my turning point as many might think. My turning point had come years earlier as I began to feel on fire for what I was learning. That night was not my turning point, but my ignition point. I felt I would burst if I did not start shouting out the truth. A truth that too many of us still feel the need to whisper and lock away, while the world shouts us down with lies.

I knew it was time for me to find my voice… lest the stars and the rocks cry out in my place. Open your eyes; look around! He is here… enthroned in the circle above the earth... I Am!

final thoughts

There was a time when we all believed. We were not so "educated." Our intellect didn't allow us to ignore the Creator. The evidence was too overwhelming. The Heavens declared the Glory of God… the skies proclaimed the work of His hands (Psalm 19:1)… and we listened. Then as our intellect grew, our wisdom diminished. As we began to think we knew best and had a better way, God no longer mattered. Lies became truth until the truth was no longer recognizable. We've lost our way, but the story doesn't end there. There is a pathway home and the light of Jesus still shines to show us the way.

I was able to find my way to redemption because I was blessed with the opportunity to grow up in a home of extraordinary Christian faith. During my childhood, the majority of the population had a faith in God and in Christ, the Son; unfortunately, that is no longer true. As my book made its way through the editorial process, my editor reminded me, "Others might be searching for direction and having trouble finding it on their own. In addition to your story, this book needs to offer them a clear path to redemption." I asked him to share his thoughts. It is our prayer that the following words will guide you on your personal journey to know Jesus better.

YOUR OWN STORY OF REDEMPTION

There is one God and you were in close relationship with Him until you discovered and chose to travel the road of sin. Every lie you tell, every hateful attitude you exhibit, every sexual sin that you engage in, every self-centered action, and every moral compromise pushes you farther from your Creator. God refers to these actions and attitudes as "sin," and we're all guilty.

The Apostle Paul says it this way, "For all have sinned and fall short of the glory of God" (Romans 3:23).

God is not content to let His relationship with you slip away. He has initiated a means of repairing the broken relationship. The solution for your sin problem meant the death of God's only Son, Jesus Christ. Through His death on a Roman cross, you now have a bridge back into a healthy relationship with God.

The Apostle Paul again says, "Therefore, since we have been justified through faith, we have peace with God through our Lord Jesus Christ, through whom we have gained access by faith into this grace in which we now stand" (Romans 5:1, 2).

In order to cross the bridge that Jesus built by His death and resurrection, you must take responsibility for your past and surrender your future into God's gracious hands. Here's how:

Believe that Jesus has done enough to save you. "And without faith it is impossible to please God, because anyone who comes to him must believe that he exists and that he rewards those who earnestly seek him" (Hebrews 11:6).

Turn away from sin and commit to following Jesus. This is called repentance. "In the past God overlooked such ignorance, but now he commands all people everywhere to repent" (Acts 17:30).

Step down from the throne of your heart and let Jesus reign over your life. "That if you confess with your mouth, 'Jesus is Lord,' and believe in your heart that God raised him from the dead, you will be saved" (Romans 10:9).

Imitate the death, burial, and resurrection of Jesus through baptism (immersion) in water. "We were therefore buried with him through baptism into death in order that, just as Christ was raised from the dead through the glory of the Father, we too may live a new life" (Romans 6:4).

Once across God's bridge of salvation, all of your past sins are washed away and you receive God's Holy Spirit to guide you into a life that honors God and reflects your gratitude to Jesus. "Peter replied, 'Repent and be baptized, every one of you, in the name of Jesus Christ for the forgiveness of your sins. And you will receive the gift of the Holy Spirit'" (Acts 2:38).

Your story of redemption could begin today.

www.ingramcontent.com/pod-product-compliance
Lightning Source LLC
LaVergne TN
LVHW051102080426
835508LV00019B/2014